- Inspirations From Scotland
Edited by Aimée Vanstone

 Young Writers

First published in Great Britain in 2005 by:
Young Writers
Remus House
Coltsfoot Drive
Peterborough
PE2 9JX
Telephone: 01733 890066
Website: www.youngwriters.co.uk

SB ISBN 1 84602 235 5

Foreword

Young Writers was established in 1991 and has been passionately devoted to the promotion of reading and writing in children and young adults ever since. The quest continues today. Young Writers remains as committed to the fostering of burgeoning poetic and literary talent as ever.

This year's Young Writers competition has proven as vibrant and dynamic as ever and we are delighted to present a showcase of the best poetry from across the UK. Each poem has been carefully selected from a wealth of *Playground Poets* entries before ultimately being published in this, our thirteenth primary school poetry series.

Once again, we have been supremely impressed by the overall high quality of the entries we have received. The imagination, energy and creativity which has gone into each young writer's entry made choosing the best poems a challenging and often difficult but ultimately hugely rewarding task - the general high standard of the work submitted amply vindicating this opportunity to bring their poetry to a larger appreciative audience.

We sincerely hope you are pleased with our final selection and that you will enjoy *Playground Poets - Inspirations From Scotland* for many years to come.

Contents

Hannah Barnett (11)   17
Alice Lindley (11)   18

Collydean Primary School, Collydean
Niall Maynes (11)   18
Emma Robertson (11)   18
Jack Thomson (11)   19
Chelsie Courts (11)   19
Stephanie Arnott (11)   20
Shannon Blackwood (11)   20
Kari Stenhouse (11)   21
Michelle Proudfoot (11)   21
Farhan Ahmed (11)   22

Crossroads Primary School, Keith
Erik Francis (10)   22
Matthew Evans (10)   23
Eleanor Green (10)   23
Rosie Russell (11)   24
Hayleigh Mackinnon (10)   25
Jacqueline Taylor (12)   26

Duncow Primary School, Kirkmahoe
Jessica Martin (8)   26
Lisa Fergusson (9)   27
Josh Patterson (9)   27

Dunning Primary School, Dunning
Amye Dolby (10)   28
Calum Law (11)   28
Cameron McLeay (11)   28
Hamish Maguire (11)   29
Kayleigh McLeish (10)   29

Fencedyke Primary School, Bourtreehill
Laura To (7)   29
Chloë Leggat (9)   30
Heather Laing (10)   30
Stuart Fairgrieve (9)   31
Nicole Rose (9)   31

Christina Menzies (9)	32
Kieran Sharpe (9)	32
Nathanael McEwan (10)	33
Courtney Picken (9)	33
Jade Gorman (10)	34
Steven Black (10)	34
Connor McCormick (9)	34
Matthew McFarlane (9)	35
Adele Clarke (9)	35
Chloe Reilly (10)	35
Connor McLaughlin (9)	36
Laura Sinclair (9)	36
Lauren Beattie (10)	37
Richard McNeil (9)	37
Jenifer Russell (9)	38
Jordon Tennant (10)	38
Kerrie Duff (10)	39
Daniel McNeil (10)	39
Shannon Bowie (10)	40
Chelsie Watson (9)	40
Elizabeth Gray (10)	41
Peter Fulton (10)	41
Kimberly McLaughlin (11)	42
Nica Burns (10)	42
Julie Davidson (10)	43
Rachel To (11)	43
Rachael Allan (11)	44
Scott Baillie (10)	44
Kirsty Hart (11)	45
Dale Brown (11)	45
Melissa Todd (11)	46
Sheridan Russell (10)	46
Jaspreet Singh (11)	47
Tamara McCartney (10)	47
Toni McGookin (10)	48
George Lawson (8)	48
Arran Watt (7)	48
Alexander Taylor (10)	49
Declan Hunter (11)	49
Jamie Wilson (7)	49
Jenn Matthews (10)	50
Rebecca Johnston (10)	51

Elliott Skeoch (7)   52
Abbie Laing (7)   52
Liam Fitzsimmons (7)   52
Luke McNeil (7)   53
Scott McKie (7)   53
Louise Morrison (10)   54
Callum Reilly (7)   54
Malcolm West (7)   55
Ross Skivington (7)   55
Leon Hendry (7)   55
Ashley Wilson (7)   56
Robbie Taylor (7)   56
Christopher Gunn (7)   56
Haven-Lee Walker (7)   57
Leah Hamilton (7)   57
Toni Morgan (8)   57
Ellie McTear (7)   58
Callum Drysdale (10)   58
Natasha Duncan (7)   59
Carly McGowan (7)   59
Shannon Flynn (7)   59
Megan Donnelly (10)   60
Zoe Jardine (10)   60
Lorin Kirk (11)   61
Emma Strachan (11)   61

Fishermoss Primary School, Portlethen
Megan Shearer (8)   62
Charlotte Torrance (8)   62
Kirsty Duncan (8)   63

Golfhill Primary School, Airdrie
Keiran De La Mare (9)   63
Calum Paterson (8)   64
Jack Black (8)   64

Kinnoull Primary School, Perth
Kirsty Irvine (10)   65
Holly Buchanan (10)   66
Sylvie Kay (11)   67

Ciara Hayes (11)   68
Catriona Anderson (10)   69

Ladybank Primary School, Ladybank
Emili Harris (9)   69
Eilidh Lewis (9)   70
Katie Coull (10)   71
Siobhan Laing (9)   71
Steven Anderson (10)   72
Cameron Brown (9)   72
Bethany Smith (9)   73
Sean Brown (11)   73
Christopher Royle (9)   74
Caitlin Self (10)   74
Aaron Shand (9)   75
Alasdair Robertson (9)   75
Kelly Martin (12)   75
Josh Whitelaw (9)   76
Jonathan Simpson (10)   76

Ladyton Primary School, Bonhill
Amanda Melville (12)   77
Samantha Davidson (10)   78
Alexander Dow (11)   78
Emma Evans (10)   79
Shannon McKeown (11)   79
Chloe Beck (11)   80
Jacqueline Moir (12)   80
Loren McCuish (10)   81
Kayleigh Roberts (11)   81

Luss Primary School, Luss
Ellie Scott (10)   82
Stephy Woods (10)   82
Rhianna Baxter (10)   82
Sean McPhail (10)   83
Alice Rankin (11)   83
Robbie Anderson (11)   83
Hayley Gray (11)   84
Hamish Marsh (11)   84

Macduff School, Macduff

Stacy Thomson (12)	85
Leona McKenzie (12)	86
Amanda Watt (12)	87
James Geddes (11)	88
Danielle Murdoch (11)	89
Ellie Wiseman (11)	90
Debbie Fowlie (12)	91
Chelsea Barber (12)	91
Amber Lorimer (11)	92
Louise Mackinnon (11)	93

Mill O' Forest Primary School, Stonehaven

Emily Coleman (11)	93
Caitlyn Cheyne (11)	94
Danny Malcolm (11)	94
Daniel Paterson (11)	95
Jamie Andrew (11)	95
Stewart Clark (12)	96
Stuart Saville (11)	96
Eilish Baird (12)	97
Emma Gordon & Rhys Falconer (9)	97
Deborah Ogilvie (10)	98
Kelly Muir (12)	98
Billy Wilson (9)	99
Ethan Attwood (11)	99
Kim Mellis (10)	99
Chloe Jackson (10)	100
Kelly McLaren (10)	100
Ryan Brown (9)	100
Rebecca McRobbie (10)	101
Sophie Christie (10)	101
Tonicha Masson (9)	101
John Campbell (10)	102
Kieran Paley (10)	102
Connor Douglas (9) & Gemma Brown (11)	102
Euan Dryburgh (10)	103
Katie Gordon (9)	103
Andrew Dart (10)	104
Cheri Brown (10)	104
Sam Gutteridge (11)	105

Shannon Smith (9)	106
Kirsty Thomson (9)	106
Kieran Johnson (9)	106
Jonathan Penman (9)	107
Rachael Craig (9)	107
Lee Ramage (10)	107
Denzel Bruce (10)	108
Stuart Moir (9)	108
Charlie Malcolm (10)	108
Tara Hector (9)	109
Caitlin Imray (10)	109
Zoe Davidson (9)	109
Lauren Gerrard (11)	110
Christopher Hunt (11)	110
Rachel Eastcroft (10)	110
Jenni Ogg (10)	111
Chloe Christie (10)	111
Craig Forbes (10)	111
Francesca Ballard (11)	112
Greig Clark (11)	112
Michelle Ingram (11)	113
Murray Cheyne (10)	113
James Johnson (10)	114
Scott Webster (10)	114
Gemma Gerrard (11)	115
Robyn Munro (11)	115
Zoe Taylor (10)	116
Becky Bruce (11)	116
Ashleigh Hunter (11)	116
David Craigmyle (10)	117

Nethermains Primary School, Denny

Alan Rae (8)	117
Daniel Guy (9)	117
Mairi Soldatic (8)	118
Christopher Mullan (8)	118
Caitlyn Ross (8)	118
Nicole Wilson (9)	119
Emma Wilson (9)	119
Amy Weir (8)	119
Jordan Mitchell (8)	120

Charley Shanks (9)   120
Hannah Shade (8)   120
Lauren Baillie (11)   121
Robert Macalister (10)   121
Terri Valentine (11)   121
Caroline Docherty (10)   122
Cameron Sweeney (10)   122
David Gemmell (10)   122
Linzi Davidson (11)   123
Jodie Kane (11)   123
Danielle McAteer (10)   123
Daryl MacMillan (10)   124
Craig Fulton (10)   124
Gary Collier (10)   124
Alexander Fullard (10)   125
Daniel McPhillips (11)   125
Jacqueline Huskie (11)   125
Jodie Butler (12)   126
Argyle Ryan (12)   126
Ross McNeil (12)   127
Jayjay Allen (9)   127
Stacie Hunter (12)   128
Liam Wright (11)   128
Siobhan Clark (11)   129
Emma Marshall (11)   130
Taylor Brown (12)   130
Colin Mackay (12)   131
Scot Cameron (11)   131

Newarthill Primary School, Newarthill
Rhys Park (11)   132
Sarah Smith (11)   132
Abigail Grover (11)   133
Kirstin Donnelly (11)   133
Emma King (11)   134
Allyson Stevely (11)   134
Brian Flynn (11)   135
Tiffany Matthews (11)   135
Laura Hill (11)   136
Nicola Blair (11)   136
Adee Cook (12)   137

Colleen Hughes (11)   137
Fiona Wellcoat (11)   138
Jason Hattie (11)   139
Aryana Motaghian (11)   140

New Elgin Primary School, New Elgin
Grant Rollo (10)   140
Robert Forsyth (9)   141
Ellice McCart (9)   141
Danielle Newlands (10)   142
Abbie McKillop (9)   142
Jack Byiers (9)   143
Arran Johnston (10)   143
Blair Johnston (10)   144
Sophie Fraser (9)   144
Billie Slinn (10)   145
John Stuart (10)   145
Shawn Sinclair (9)   146
Michael Armstrong (10)   146
Paige Cameron (10)   147
Jade Young (9)   147
Greg Gallacher (10)   148
Angela Adam (9)   148

Pennyland Primary School, Thurso
Drew Crawford (11)   149
Aaron Taylor (9)   149
Andrew McKay (10)   150
Matthew Hardman (11)   150
Cameron Laidlaw (10)   150
Sarah Douglas (10)   151
Hannah Smith (10)   151
Gemma Mackay (10)   152
Gemma Strange (10)   152
Fraser Baxter (9)   153
Jack Dunnett (9)   153
Amelia Mackay (9)   154
Stacey Fry (10)   154
Lewis Maclellan (9)   155
Leanne Maclean (9)   155
Ashley McPhee (11)   156

Jamie Lawrie (11)   156
Danielle Hawken (10)   157
Shannon Fulton (10)   157

Philiphaugh Community School, Selkirk
Sam Berry (10)   157
Nicola Dehnolm (11)   158
Annabel Watson (10)   158
Danny Brown (11)   158
Stuart Hislop (10)   158
Lee McCudden (10)   159
Matthew Valentine (10)   159

Rockfield Primary School, Oban
Craig Wright (11)   159
Lauren Smith (11)   160
Nicola Burgar (11)   160
Aidan Harris (12)   160
Anna Smith (12)   161
Katy Melville (11)   161
Pamela Macnab (11)   161
Marcus Ward (11)   162
James Milligan (11)   162
Chloe Brown (11)   163
Rebekah MacFarlane (11)   163
Rachel Broadfoot (11)   164
Rowen MacAskill (11)   164

St Gabriel's RC School, Prestonpans
Robbie Wood (8)   165
Jade McAlpine (8)   165
Mikey Hamilton (9)   165
Derryn Dryburgh   166
Paige Cummings (9)   166
Liam Storrie (8)   166
Darren Halliday (8)   167
Nicollette Blair (9)   167
Erin Scott (9)   167
Chloe Fraser (8)   168
Declan Luby (8)   168

Tyler Byrne (9)	168
Ryan Turner (8)	169
Stuart Tait (8)	169
Joanne Clelland (8)	169
Kieran Cowan (9)	170
Holly Bye (8)	170
Erin Connachan (9)	170
Kayleigh Houston (8)	171
Connor Horrocks (8)	171
Adam Connolly (8)	171
Josie Adams (8)	172
Liam Tervet (8)	172
Patrick McLaren (8)	172
Louis McCabe (8)	173
Samara Hunter (8)	173

St John's Primary School, Blackwood

Josin Jose (8)	173
Sophia Glanville (8)	174
Olivia Glanville (10)	174
Daniel Lafferty (8)	175
Sean Tierney (8)	175
Fraser Munro (9)	176
Michael Marra (9)	176
Lee Hughes (8)	176
Paula Lavery (8)	177
Ben Gallacher (10)	177
Saranne Hamilton (9)	177
Lee McInally (9)	178
Darren Dearie (9)	178
Lisa Law (9)	178

St Mary's RC Primary School, Bathgate

Kirsten MacDonald (9)	179
Nicola Reynolds (8)	179
Andrew Shedden (8)	180
Cormac Hughes (8)	180
Louise Burns (8)	181
Caitlin McKenna (8)	181
Eva Doolan (9)	182
Kieran Boyle (8)	182

Lisa Manson (9)   183
Daniel Copeman (8)   183
Shanna Smith (8)   184
Marie McLaughlin (8)   184
Youssef Bel Abbes (8)   184
Robbie Copeman (8)   185

St Ninian's RC Primary School, Menzieshill
Lee Thomson (8)   185
Tori-Jade Hodgson (8)   185
Stevyn Wilkinson (11)   186
Kirstie McAulay (10)   186
Olivia Marr (11)   187
Karli Webster (10)   187
Rachel Cameron (11)   188
Cameron Conway (10)   188
Elise Wilson (11)   189
Josh Bray (10)   190
Kelsey Gowans (8)   190
Shaun Thain (11)   191
Shaun Wilkinson (8)   191
Kayleigh Papendorf (9)   191
Cameron McGregor (8)   192
Lucy Smith (8)   192

Sciennes Primary School, Edinburgh
Mary Pearson (10)   192
Amirah Ahmed (11) & Natalie Prosser (10)   193
Kirstie-Ann McPherson (11)   193
Mairi Cross (10)   194
Sophie Devlin (10)   194
Iain Brown (11)   194
Richard Ellis, Toby McClorey (10) & Abdullah Muaqat (11)   195
Kirsten MacFarlane & Jonathan Robertson (10)   195
Tom Walker, Oh-Heon Kwon (10) & Anna Purdom (11)   195

Stobhill Primary School, Gorebridge
Leon Miller (8)   196
Samantha McColm (8)   196
Emma Cullen (8)   196
Paige Watson (8)   197

Dale Cummings (8)	197
Abbey Rutherford (8)	197
Chanel Drysdale (8)	198
Sam Fisher (8)	198
Emma Wilson (8)	198
Chloe Hutchison (8)	199
Joel Urquhart (8)	199
Erin Flanagan (8)	199
Rachel Robertson (8)	200
Lori McVittie (8)	200

Strone Of Cally Primary School, Bridge of Cally

Cole McCulloch (8)	201
Connor Blanche (11)	202
William Blanche (9)	203
Harris McCulloch (9)	204
Callum Rimmer (9)	204
Lewis Crichton (9)	205

Whitecross Primary School, Whitecross

Kiera McKimm (6)	205
Craig Lang (7)	206
Cameron Marshall (7)	206
Iain Parkinson (7)	206
Steven Ramage (7)	207
Kevin Struthers (7)	207
Chelsea Forbes (6)	207
Fiona Parkinson (7)	208
Georgia Brodie (6)	208

The Poems

Light And Dark Poem

The light scares the darkness,
Right out of the way.
The dark hides in shadows,
All through the day.
Some people find it scary,
Dark through the air.
So the light scares it away,
So everything's fair.
The light scares the dark,
And the dark scares the light,
And so that's why we have
The day and the night.
During the day the dark hides away,
And so the light keeps it at bay.
The dark hides in the shadows,
It stays away,
Just to come out when the light goes away.
For the light cannot stay, there's simply no way,
It goes away to the other side of the bay.
So the dark it appears,
It's some people's fears.
It fills the air,
It gives people a scare.
So while the light's away all during the night,
The dark is giving people a terrible fright.
But the light will come back,
Give the darkness the sack and the
Dark will go back to the shadows all day.

Sam Williams (11)
Barthol Chapel School, Barthol Chapel

Gymnastics

G ymnastics is fun
Y ou've got to save your strength
M y mum coaches gymnastics
N umb body straight after
A nd I have skill
S pins are easy moves
T here are four pieces
I am smart at gymnastics
C ompetitions are exciting
S ome tumbles are hard and some are easy.

Lee-Ann Donald (10)
Barthol Chapel School, Barthol Chapel

Riddle

I would be a black spot
If I stood on chalk
If I had no wings
I would be called a walk
I like things that are sweet
But I cannot eat
What am I?
. . . I am a fly.

Callum Keys (11)
Barthol Chapel School, Barthol Chapel

Riddle?

You can see it,
But you can't feel it,
You can make it,
But you can't sell it,
It can grow beneath trees,
But you can't pick it.

. . . Shadow.

Jamie Booth (11)
Barthol Chapel School, Barthol Chapel

My Idol

My idol's not in music,
If he was he wouldn't be an acoustic,
His name doesn't sound British,
He's actually fully Scottish,
His pay-job isn't round,
Nor is his job flat,
They say his job's an art,
An art that he has got,
Alright, alright I'll give you a clue,
But it's not a clue if you know who,
His sport's got a ball
And it's not football,
But it may be no use at all,
Because you probably haven't heard of him;
That's all!
Who is it?

Marcus Di Rollo.

Jack Chalmers (11)
Barthol Chapel School, Barthol Chapel

How To Make A Beanstalk

One whole cow,
A boy called Jack,
A handful of beans held in a sack,
A sad, unhappy mum,
With no food to give her son.

Sell the cow,
To get the handful of beans held in a sack,
Give them to unhappy Mum
She'll throw the beans out of the window
After thirty days and thirty nights,
You will have a tall green beanstalk.

Angus Bruce-Gardner (10)
Barthol Chapel School, Barthol Chapel

Power Cut

I'm in my bed the power goes off,
I hear a sound coming from the loft
I'm terrified,
Yes, petrified.

I call, 'Mum, Mum I got a fright
The power's gone out of the night light.'
'Don't worry it will be back on soon.'
'But it doesn't light up my room.'

Then at 2 o'clock
I heard a knock
I got a candle, I used its light,
I glimpsed a shadow in the night.

'Mum are we going to be attacked?
Because it really is very black.'
'Don't worry, it's back on now,
Go to bed and count the cows!'

Kieran Booth (9)
Barthol Chapel School, Barthol Chapel

The Missing House

I see it every night,
When the moon isn't very bright,
There are no street lamps, so it isn't light.

The big grey steps *aren't* inviting,
And an oil lamp isn't good lighting,
The number 39 is in weird writing.

It isn't really there at all,
There is only the old town hall,
Where people dance and have a ball.

It isn't really there at all,
It isn't really there at all,
It isn't really there at all.

Jamie Rodgers (9)
Barthol Chapel School, Barthol Chapel

The Hungbunglee

The Hungbunglee is a monstrous creature
And he is definitely not a preacher.
He doesn't come out at day, but night,
And isn't afraid to put up a fight.

We always say he's rather cute,
Because of his little furry suit.
He has three gigantic eyes
That sometimes scare tough guys.
He has small arms that become big,
Which comes in useful when it wants to dig.
It has big teeth and claws,
Which are just as sharp as saws.
It is red with green spots,
Which are brighter than fluorescent dots.

You'll know when he's coming because you'll hear
These horrible sounds that will fill you with fear.
First you'll hear two beats of a drum,
And then there'll be a low-pitched hum.
Then there'll be a loud buzz,
But then you'll see a complete fuzz
Because you've just been eaten by the Hungbunglee,
He'll come after you, like he came after me.

Jamie Strathearn (9)
Barthol Chapel School, Barthol Chapel

Riddle

There are four of them,
Some are hot, some are cold
Blossom flows through the trees
Leaves fall, some flowers grow on a wall,
Children in a paddling pool
What is it?
. . . Seasons.

Emma Simpson (8)
Barthol Chapel School, Barthol Chapel

Watsebacers

They look small
You may think that they're weak but they're strong,
They're small and fast to get away from killers.
You find them in tree houses big or small,
On the top of trees, they're light and soft and fluffy.
They swing from vine to vine.
You may wonder how they get to their houses.
There are gaps in the trees that they go through.
They make the stairs by stone that they have carved with other
stones.
There are platforms that they walk on, the leader wears a dead
bird's head.
The other ones wear fabric.
They fight with stones and twigs and vine!

Kieran Wilson (9)
Barthol Chapel School, Barthol Chapel

Desert

The sun beating down, blazing, blinding,
The tumbleweed intertwining,
Far away trekking over the sand,
The golden hills are just more land,
You feel all weak,
Your sweatbands leak.

There's nowhere to hide,
It's all a big ride,
There's a small waterhole,
A desert is the opposite from cold,
A camel can be very small,
But the hump on its back is tall.

Charlotte Cooke (9)
Barthol Chapel School, Barthol Chapel

Ancient Egyptians

Ancient Egyptians making pyramids for pharaohs,
Worshipping cats wherever they go.
According to them they are fluffy gods from the desert
Ancient Egypt is where the cat with a hat sat in the middle of Cairo.
Tombs used for pharaohs and queens.
In ancient Egypt people are soldiers, tomb builders and craftsmen.
Egyptian deserts are dry with sand dunes all around,
Sandstorms rage and blast through the deserts,
And all the scorpions hide in scrubs and lizards on rocks.

Drew Cowie (10)
Barthol Chapel School, Barthol Chapel

Flower Opera

Left on the playground all alone
Sitting on a great big stone.
Looking at the clouds go by
Like candyfloss to the untrained eye.

I hear a whistling sound
So I look to the ground, I see
A thing so wondrous
A litter of buds whistling and over in the corner there
The bluebells are ringing, the daffodils singing.

It is not just a beautiful sight
But a beautiful smell
The colours jingling around.

But the bell rings
I look away
When I look back
They are frozen.

Jena Brennan (10)
Carnbroe Primary School, Coatbridge

My Imagination Football Game

When I have nothing to do
I dream and imagine a football game playing.
The Underground Vs the Enchanted.

The floodlights show red and black
For the Underground to win.
The ball is a head, the goalposts are bones
And there is a web in it for the net.

At the other side there are wands for goalposts
And mystical lines.
The floodlights show blue and green
For the Enchanted.

But really I am sitting down on the ground
Staring into space.
Bored to death in the real world.

Ross Cairns (9)
Carnbroe Primary School, Coatbridge

A Rainbow For A Crown

The trees stand up in the sky
With a rainbow for a crown
The fence stands like an army
The snake slithers about
When the kids are playing in the playground
With the wind that sneaks about
When the sun comes out
And realises we're happy
When it's night the stars shine bright
The playground shines like a diamond
With the air that's in the light
When day comes back
The school bell rings
Then we're playing games
The birds are lighting up the playground
While they're singing away.

Dayna Hughes (10)
Carnbroe Primary School, Coatbridge

What Can You . . .?

Look, what can you see?

Mark smiling
Sean swinging
Jena jumping.

Listen, what can you hear?

Heather singing
Calum joking
Dayna laughing.

Smell, what can you smell?

Ashley's hairspray
Alana's perfume
Lauren's make-up.

Taste, what can you taste?

Lilly's bad breath
Shannon's lipstick
Johnny's hairgel.

Touch, what can you touch?

Greg's glasses
Natasha's bobble
Ross' pencil.

Wear, what can you wear?

Craig's T-shirt
Bethany's shoes
Leanne's socks.

Lucy Wright (9)
Carnbroe Primary School, Coatbridge

The Football Way

A hotshot goal we got when it rolled behind the line
With my mate in a celebration
We skidded across the grass
Jumped in our jerseys
We landed in a chant with green stains on our knees.

Back to the midway line running like tiger sharks
Loosened legs like a newly oiled screw
A thudding heart
Like a hammer to a nail
I think we all had that from the way we were playing.

We won the ball
The centre mid took it by two
And made a runner of a pass to the left winger
And it went all the way to the right winger
Who crossed it in
And the forward nodded it in
With a great header!

And then the final whistle blew.

Greg Smith (9)
Carnbroe Primary School, Coatbridge

Eco School

We are an eco school.
We're better than anyone because we're totally cool.

We have a new thing called name and shame
Because people drop their litter so they're the ones to blame.

Our playground isn't that big.
But since we are an eco school we can play tig.

We like to recycle stuff,
The eco patrol is very tough.

We hand out competitions at the end of the day.
When the school bell rings everybody shouts *'Hooray!'*

The school has an eco song
But I must say it isn't very long.

So you see we are healthy
Our children are quite wealthy.

If we don't get our second flag before I go into high school,
That wouldn't be cool.

Bethanie Knowles (9)
Carnbroe Primary School, Coatbridge

What Are Friends?

What makes friends?
Love
Life and
Family.

Love is from your heart
May it be a mum, a dad or a sister
Love isn't a thing that you want to be lost
Love might be an auntie, an uncle or brother
Love is from deep inside your heart
A sport that is special to everybody.

Life is delicate, it can be lost very easily
May it be a tree, a squirrel or a human
Life holds feelings, sadness, happiness or jealousy.

Your friends are not just one of these
They are everything you desire.

      My friends.

Natasha Fox (9)
Carnbroe Primary School, Coatbridge

Music

Music is like a chunk of gold
Music is the opposite from cold
It has its lows and same for downs
But is immune to frowns
It tastes like apple
And feels like wood
But if you're not good you'll be pelted with food
You'll never meet someone who hates music
But if I do I think I will lose it.

Jareth Cameron (11)
Colliston Primary School, Colliston

Different Kinds Of Music

Music could be slow,
Could be medium,
Could be fast
It could be low
But you could still have a laugh.
Music could be quiet,
Could be medium,
Could be loud
Anyway, you could still be proud.
Music could be short,
Could be medium,
Could be long,
But still always keep it on.
The music could be old,
Could be medium,
Could be new
But everyone at least has a few.
The music could have drums,
Could have violins,
Could have lyrics,
But you don't need the medics.

Donna Munro (11)
Colliston Primary School, Colliston

Music

The flute is a sweet sound but bitter,
A clarinet is a calming sound but on some notes isn't.
The piano can be scary or soothing
A drum can come in different sizes
While others only come in one size
The trumpet is a high-pitched sound
When it isn't it is a muffled sound
Music is instruments playing in a band.

Sarah Martin (10)
Colliston Primary School, Colliston

Being Scared

Being scared is hiding,
Hiding where I'm not seen.
Being scared is hiding in my bed
I'm really scared now!
I can sense something that's scary,
It moves closer and closer towards light
And gives me a very big fright!
Seeing something so scary,
Torch! Torch, I need a torch!
Could it be a monster?
Torturer?
No!
I reach out to get it,
Feels funny, woolly, cosy and scary!
It's closer now so I can sort of see it,
It's only my dad come to say goodnight!
There's nothing to be scared about!

Holly Macrae (11)
Colliston Primary School, Colliston

Christmas!

That special day comes every year
And brings around Christmas cheer
So then comes that magic day
When Santa comes on his sleigh
He leaves your presents by the fire
And soars the world
Before he retires
He takes the sherry and the pies
And a carrot for Rudolph before he flies!

Ian Reid (11)
Colliston Primary School, Colliston

Colours

Red is like anger surging through me,
It's like strawberry sauce dripping off an ice cream.

Orange is like a beach ball flying through the air,
It's like a fire flickering in the dark.

Yellow is like sand on a desert island beach,
Yellow is like custard, sometimes a treat.

Green is bright, like the fresh spring grass,
Green is dark and green is light, like leaves on trees.

Blue is like the waves lapping on the beach,
Blue is like the sky passing by us every day.

Pink is like your tongue licking up ice cream,
Pink is like the parrots flying through the trees.

April Shepherd (11)
Colliston Primary School, Colliston

Winter

Winter makes you want a hot chocolate

Winter makes you want to stay in bed

Winter makes you want it to be Christmas

Overall winter is fun.

Lewis Raffan (10)
Colliston Primary School, Colliston

I Want To Be A Vet

I want to be a vet,
So helpful and well paid
You get to help animals in need,
All the dogs, cats, rabbits, hamsters,
Oh, I would love to be a vet.

Gabrielle Thompson (11)
Colliston Primary School, Colliston

Darkness

When your mum kisses you goodnight,
And switches off the light
Darkness creeps upon you
And gives you a big *fright!*
You're there in the dark
Thinking it's going to be alright
Tick-tock, tick-tock
Phew, it's just the clock
Drip . . . drip . . . drip
Oh my gosh!
What is that?
I find my courage
And shut my eyes
And try not to think of the dangers inside
I wake up and it's morning
And am glad to say it is
But I dread the night ahead of me.

Claire Simpson (10)
Colliston Primary School, Colliston

Dogs

Dogs can be big or small,
A Great Dane is very tall,
A guide dog helps the blind,
A boxer has a very good mind,
A terrier has an awful bite,
A St Bernard has very good sight
Now you can see
How great dogs can be.

Elizabeth Webster (11)
Colliston Primary School, Colliston

Bubblegum

B ubblegum soft and chewy
U nder the wrapping sweet and juicy
B races are off, what do I do?
B ubblegum, oh! bubblegum, I'll come to buy you.
L ong, sticky, chewy bubblegum
E very kind of gum, I ask my mum to buy me more.
G reat, long, stretchy bubblegum
U nder the wrapping sweet and juicy
M um please buy me some more.

Laura Blake (12)
Colliston Primary School, Colliston

Sisters

S isters can be nasty but also fun
I t's cool to get presents from her
S isters aren't cool when they break doors
T o fight with my sister is the worst crime ever
E ven if I am sad, she still makes me special
R eady to argue any time
S he awaits a little fight.

Courtney Morgan (12)
Colliston Primary School, Colliston

Rabbits

R ough or soft
A crobatic
B iting at the wire to get out
B ubbly and fun
I love to play with rabbits
T hey are so much fun
S oft and cuddly.

Hannah Barnett (11)
Colliston Primary School, Colliston

Noise

Noise, he likes to shout a lot,
Being quiet, he does not.
He very much likes to shout.
He also loves to dance about
He screams and squeals in people's ears
He's been around for many years.
He likes to creep and scare the boys
That's my favourite type of noise.

Alice Lindley (11)
Colliston Primary School, Colliston

Rabbits

R is for runs joined onto the big red hutch
A is for all rabbits, they are so small and cute
B is for Brownie, my rabbit's mum
B is for blue like my rabbit's food bowl
 I is for inside the hutch, lovely and cosy and layered with hay
T is for Ted, my rabbit's name
S is for straw that they sleep on.

Niall Maynes (11)
Collydean Primary School, Collydean

Emma's Parrot

Autumn is very cute,
He has a red, red shoot,
He can say lots of words,
Unlike any other birds,
He climbs up his cage and
Then gets a rage.

Emma Robertson (11)
Collydean Primary School, Collydean

The Natural World

T is for trees, our wonderful trees,
H is for humans with shoulders and knees,
E is for elephants' very long trunks.

N is for Norway, the Vikings really stunk,
A is for Africa, tall trees and giraffes,
T is for Tundra where you need to wear hats,
U is for underground, good for growing sprouts,
R is for rams, that look much like goats,
A is for Arctic polar bears and moose,
L is for life, lots of births and deaths.

W is for whales, big and hungry,
O is for octopus, slimy and inky,
R is for rocks, big and heavy,
L is for light, the sun big and bright,
D is for darkness, it's as dark as night.

The natural world.

Jack Thomson (11)
Collydean Primary School, Collydean

My Cat Chelsie

M y cat is black and white
Y ou have to be careful when you play with her or she might bite.

C helsie is really playful
A nd she loves to play with things like string.
T ummy rubbing, she hates so much.

C helsie is a lovely cat
H er coat is so soft
E veryone loves her
L ots of people think she is sweet
S he is a house cat
I love her lots
E veryone likes my cat Chelsie.

Chelsie Courts (11)
Collydean Primary School, Collydean

My Pet Rabbit

I once had a lovely pet rabbit
He was fluffy and not ever crabbit
He always played fetch with me
And once tried to play with a bee
I knew him for almost five years
I knew all his frights and bad fears
He had a bad fall
And banged into a wall
We took him to the vet
And I made a bet that he would live
But I had to say bye-bye
'Cause now he's away to that hutch in the sky
I miss him so, so much
Just looking at that empty hutch.

Stephanie Arnott (11)
Collydean Primary School, Collydean

My Granny

My granny is wonderful, pretty and kind
If I make a mistake she doesn't mind
When I fall in puddles
She helps me up and gives me loads of cuddles.

She bakes stuff with me
And makes me a delicious tea
She takes me places
And buys me strawberry laces.

I love her so much
Luckily she doesn't live in a hutch
She loves me too
And her friend is called Sue.

Shannon Blackwood (11)
Collydean Primary School, Collydean

Ted

My kitten is called Ted,
He's so cute when he sleeps in his bed.
He has a tiny little head,
My mum fell in love with him in a second.
She would have ignored him if it wasn't for me whinging,
I wouldn't be here with Ted today.

During the day he goes a tad crazy,
He jumps a far distance with his head high.
But then he needs a rest, he gets out of breath,
He goes through to the kitchen.
He catches his eye on a mitten,
Then runs through in a hyper mood.
And in a second he's up in Heaven,
Dreaming of hopefully us!

Kari Stenhouse (11)
Collydean Primary School, Collydean

Kittens

Kittens are filled with so much fun,
Sleeping, eating, then off they run.
Playing and jumping with their ball,
Dancing and prancing until they fall.
Munching and crunching up their food,
Making so much noise it must be good.
They settle down in a heap,
Then curl up and go to sleep!
Kittens are loveable and adorably sweet,
The most huggable pets you'll ever meet.

Michelle Proudfoot (11)
Collydean Primary School, Collydean

Ice Fire

The dragon who breathes fire
Kills and tortures
Ice fire goes into war with
Fire springing in every direction
He's got a Mohican with red skin
He thumps and bashes things in his own way
He has barbecues to roast and grill
He smirks when he is flying in the air
Whoosh, whoosh in the air with his little teddy bear!
He is tired after a long day's work, *zzzzzz*.

Farhan Ahmed (11)
Collydean Primary School, Collydean

The Playground In The Spring

I sit on the bench in the playground
In the scorching hot sun.
The sky full of big fluffy clouds
Like a big white room.

Flowers sprouting in dark flower beds,
Crawling up the big blue trellis.
I can smell the delicious fish and chips
Coming from the kitchen.

Newborn lambs jumping around
Baaing their heads off.
Baby birds getting their first flight,
Flying in little circles in the big blue sky.

Children running around mad
Screaming like monkeys playing.
All the time the sun burns in the sky
But no one notices it.

Erik Francis (10)
Crossroads Primary School, Keith

The Playground In Summer

I am in the playground on a hot, sweaty afternoon in summer.
The sun is burning like a big ball of gas flaming billions of miles away,
Touching me with its warmth.

The sunlight sizzles the leaves.
The smell of Mary's freshly baked food makes my mouth water.
Sweaty children are playing happily.

It feels like everything is melting.
Cars with their windows down are passing backwards
And forwards.

All that's being done is movement,
bees are buzzing, collecting nectar from flower to flower.
I am full of joy and happy as ever.
I can hear the big, loud ring from the bell.

Matthew Evans (10)
Crossroads Primary School, Keith

Harvest

Harvest has come and people aren't glum
They're picking and the kids are hiding and kicking
The potatoes are being pulled from the soft brown ground,
While the cutters on the combine are going round and round.
The golden wheat is being cut, so much of it the barn door won't
                                                        shut.
Lots and lots of golden grain, just make sure it doesn't rain.
Now it is the feast where we all meet, lots of grapes and bread to eat.
All the men are drinking beer, I hope we have a harvest like this
                                                        next year.

Eleanor Green (10)
Crossroads Primary School, Keith

The Playground In Summer

I am standing in the playground
On a bright, warm summer's day.
The warm breeze is blowing my
Hair ever so slightly so it tickles
The back of my neck,
Like a very soft feather.

The bees buzz round my head excitedly
And then off to find more sweet-smelling flowers
In our colourful flowery garden.

The faint bleating of faraway sheep
As they graze quite happily
On the colourful hillside,
And the cheeping of the songbirds
Fluffing up their feathers in the dried dirt,
These are the sounds of summer's nature.

Children resting, others shouting
With excitement as they play in
The full beam of the summer sun
Beating down on their exposed necks.
The bell echoes around the playground
Then quiet as we are back in class.

Rosie Russell (11)
Crossroads Primary School, Keith

Tsunami Disaster

I can see
Massive tidal waves coming towards people
Heavy waves crashing against buildings making them collapse
People running to high ground while the waves are washing
Everything away with a great force

I can hear
People screaming and crying, frightened to death
The great waves crashing against everything

I can now see
Only one palm tree and a few buildings standing
People suffering with broken hearts

I can now hear
Thousands of people have died
Very kind people have donated money
20 out of 200 islands are destroyed
There are 1.6 million people homeless

I hope that
People have shelter, food, water and medicine

I dream that none of this ever happened.

Hayleigh Mackinnon (10)
Crossroads Primary School, Keith

The Playground In Winter

I am standing in the playground, on a cold winter's day in January.
The sky is as white as a ghost
And the sun is a pale yellow.

I can hear cars crackling and crunching
On the frosty road.
People driving carefully so they don't crash.

Children are sliding excitedly on the smooth ice.
Shouting happily while falling over and laughing,
But not hurting themselves.

A sudden gust of wind makes the leaves blow up
And down,
But apart from that there was not a sound.

Jacqueline Taylor (12)
Crossroads Primary School, Keith

Earth's Pace

Oh Earth so slow,
In my dreams,
You're made of dough,
So come Earth, come with me,
For wherever I am,
I always fall on you,
On your soft, silent, gentle grass,
But when I pass,
You're always there for me,
Wherever I am,
You're always there for me.

Jessica Martin (8)
Duncow Primary School, Kirkmahoe

Down By The River

Sitting by the river
Reading a book and admiring things that live
Watching the small waves
Going through the waves,
Splash!

The birds are singing
The fish are swimming
The squirrels are up high in the trees
I can see
See all these creatures
With a lot of features
The birds sing a song
They have a sweet scent, it doesn't pong.

What could I do?
What should I do?
Should I go home
And polish the gnome
Or finish my book?
Look! Look!

I know what I'll do . . .

Lisa Fergusson (9)
Duncow Primary School, Kirkmahoe

In The Army

I like the army
Marching up and down
Going through every town
Holding a gun
Every mission accomplished
Every day and night
Fighting with all your might.

Josh Patterson (9)
Duncow Primary School, Kirkmahoe

Tony Blair

Pocket shaker
Money maker
Good times breaker
Greedy taker
Not love maker
Parliament shaker
Government breaker
War maker
Who am I?

Amye Dolby (10)
Dunning Primary School, Dunning

T-Rex - Haiku

Ancient dinosaur
Lots of teeth they weigh a lot
The king of them all.

Calum Law (11)
Dunning Primary School, Dunning

Aliens

Green and vile
Come a long mile
Slimy and grey
They're here to stay
They live in space
And have no face
What are they?

Cameron McLeay (11)
Dunning Primary School, Dunning

Car

Speed breaker
Noise maker
Petrol guzzler
Accident causer
Weighs a tonne
Great fun
What am I?

Hamish Maguire (11)
Dunning Primary School, Dunning

Curry

There was an old man from Surrey
Who served up a nice pot of curry
But when he got back
The curry was black
And he ran to the toilet in a hurry.

Kayleigh McLeish (10)
Dunning Primary School, Dunning

My Unicorn

Snow-white fluffy mane,
Sparkly horn,
Sparkles and shines
Cute pink nose,
I love it.
Sleep and dream and dream
About my unicorn, in my dream
I see my secret unicorn
Flying up in the midnight sky.

Laura To (7)
Fencedyke Primary School, Bourtreehill

Happiness

Happiness sounds like birds
Singing up in the sky
Happiness tastes like freshly
Baked bread just out the oven
Happiness feels like butterflies
Going down your body
Happiness is like getting
A new pet, a cuddly, little,
Soft, fluffy, newborn kitten.
Happiness reminds me of
My favourite dog called Zara
My gran's dog, one of my
Best friends.

Chloë Leggat (9)
Fencedyke Primary School, Bourtreehill

Happiness

Happiness tastes of fizzy things
That fizz in my mouth
Happiness sounds of tweeting birds
In a summer's sky
Happiness smells like melting chocolate
Dissolving in my mouth
Happiness feels soft
Like soft gentle flowers
Happiness looks happy
Happy as a smiling face
Happiness reminds me of fun times
With my family and friends.

Heather Laing (10)
Fencedyke Primary School, Bourtreehill

Happiness

Happiness tastes of burgers
That I eat at football matches.
Happiness smells of baked bread
That's just been freshly baked.
Happiness sounds like cheering
At football matches.
Happiness feels like I want to jump about
Like I scored the winning goal.
Happiness looks sporty and looks very, very active.
Happiness reminds me of when
I went to Disneyland and met Mickey.

Stuart Fairgrieve (9)
Fencedyke Primary School, Bourtreehill

Happiness

Happiness sounds like birds singing,
In the trees.
Happiness tastes like chocolate
Melting in the pot.
Happiness smells like baked bread
Fresh from the oven.
Happiness feels like my soft, fluffy pillow
That I hug every night.
Happiness looks like my cute teddy
That sleeps with me every night
Happiness reminds me of my family
Who love me a lot.

Nicole Rose (9)
Fencedyke Primary School, Bourtreehill

Happiness

Happiness sounds like birds
Tweeting their tunes in the morning
Happiness tastes like melting oozing chocolate
Running round your mouth
Happiness smells like flowers
Growing all over the hills and fields
Happiness feels like my favourite pillow
Smooth, soft and fluffy.
Happiness looks like a cake in a cake shop
Big and fluffy with a large sweet cherry
Happiness reminds me of the time at the fair
Going on rides enjoying myself
Happiness is like the colour pink
Like cheery cheeks on everyone.

Christina Menzies (9)
Fencedyke Primary School, Bourtreehill

Happiness

Happiness sounds like the small gentle wind,
As it blows against your face.
Happiness tastes sweet,
Like large juicy strawberries.
Happiness feels like a soft fluffy pillow,
Which I snuggle into every night.
Happiness smells like freshly baked bread,
Cooling off on your window sill.
Happiness reminds me of fun times,
Like my holiday with my family.

Kieran Sharpe (9)
Fencedyke Primary School, Bourtreehill

Darkness

Darkness sounds like a gale blowing,
Like thunder booming or waves crashing.
Darkness tastes all mouldy and wet,
Like soggy bread or sour milk.
Darkness smells of a musty grave,
Like a dead old corpse.
Darkness feels like cold, damp bread,
Like a cold, ugly man.
Darkness looks all deep and threatening,
Like something trying to get you.
Darkness reminds me of somebody's death,
Like a damp, cold grave.
Darkness tells me all the unhappy things I hate,
Like somebody telling me I'm going to die.

Nathanael McEwan (10)
Fencedyke Primary School, Bourtreehill

Happiness

Happiness sounds like the birds
Singing in the blue summer sky
Happiness tastes like sweet chocolate
Waiting to be eaten by me
Happiness smells like fresh bread
Waiting to be spread with jam
Happiness feels like soft, furry bunnies
Waiting to be cuddled by me
Happiness reminds me of my family
On fun days out at the zoo
Happiness colours can be lilac and pink
My favourite colours for happiness.

Courtney Picken (9)
Fencedyke Primary School, Bourtreehill

Happiness

Happiness sounds like birds
Singing in the bright blue sky
Happiness tastes like Cadbury's milk chocolate
Dissolving in my mouth.
Happiness smells like freshly baked bread,
With melting butter.
Happiness feels like my warm and cosy bed,
That I sleep in every night.
Happiness looks like my soft, cuddly, cute dog.
Happiness reminds me of going on holiday to Spain,
With my family.

Jade Gorman (10)
Fencedyke Primary School, Bourtreehill

Happiness

Happiness sounds like singing birds singing in the sky.
Happiness tastes like chocolate melting in your mouth.
Happiness smells like lovely flowers.
Happiness feels like you're running with your dog,
Running up and down.
Happiness looks like a lovely rainbow.
Happiness reminds me of when I got a new dog.

Steven Black (10)
Fencedyke Primary School, Bourtreehill

Sadness

Sadness sounds like dogs and people crying, tears dripping
Sadness smells like petrol, musty smells, dead plants
Sadness feels spiky, pointed, sharp, rough
Sadness looks like a waterfall of badness
Sadness reminds me of water because of the tears
Sadness tastes sour, bitter, hot.

Connor McCormick (9)
Fencedyke Primary School, Bourtreehill

Sadness

Sadness sounds like crying and moaning,
Sadness tastes sour and horrible,
Sadness smells horrid like stink bombs,
Sadness makes you feel heartbroken,
Sadness looks like something dying,
Sadness reminds me of Christmas Day when my dog died.
Sadness feels like a stick being driven through your heart.
Sadness feels bad.
Sadness is like when my bird was killed.
Sadness is when I get hurt.

Matthew McFarlane (9)
Fencedyke Primary School, Bourtreehill

Happiness

Happiness sounds like singing birds.
Happiness tastes like melting chocolate on baked toast.
Happiness smells like new carpets on our floor.
Happiness feels like a soft cuddly pup.
Happiness looks like a lovely flower on a stem.
Happiness reminds me of my family and friends.

Adele Clarke (9)
Fencedyke Primary School, Bourtreehill

Happiness

Happiness sounds like birds singing away up high in the sky
Happiness tastes like melting chocolate melting in your mouth
Happiness smells like lovely petrol going in the car
Happiness feels relaxing in the hot sun
Happiness looks exciting when the sun comes out
Happiness reminds me of my family and friends.

Chloe Reilly (10)
Fencedyke Primary School, Bourtreehill

Happiness

Happiness feels as soft
As my dog's fur,
Happiness tastes as sweet
As my gran's spaghetti Bolognese,
Happiness sounds like birds singing,
In the morning sunshine
Happiness smells like freshly baked bread,
Melting in golden, yellowy butter,
Happiness looks like the sun setting low
In the sky ready to go down,
Happiness colours are gold, yellow,
Light blue, all very bright,
Happiness reminds me of my cute dog,
All happy and well.

Connor McLaughlin (9)
Fencedyke Primary School, Bourtreehill

Happiness

Happiness sounds like birds,
Singing away up high in the beautiful sky.
Happiness tastes like chocolate,
Melting in your mouth, running about.
Happiness smells like lovely flowers
Just about to bloom.
Happiness feels like quiet,
Quiet as a baby mouse.
Happiness looks peaceful
When you're all alone.
Happiness reminds me of the sun
That looks so bright.

Laura Sinclair (9)
Fencedyke Primary School, Bourtreehill

Happiness

Happiness sounds like rain tapping
Gently on my window.
Happiness tastes sweet like chocolate
Bubbling in my mouth.
Happiness looks like a rainbow
Carved in the sky.
Happiness reminds me of my friends and family
Who I love in every way.
Happiness feels like fluffy clouds
In the sky.
Happiness smells like chocolate
Melting on toast.
Happiness gives me so much joy
I could just sing.
Happiness makes my body tingle
With enjoyment.
Happiness makes me jump so high
I am almost in the sky.
Happiness is a cloud
Full of dreams that everyone loves.

Lauren Beattie (10)
Fencedyke Primary School, Bourtreehill

Darkness

Darkness sounds like an evil laugh
As scary as death.
Darkness smells like a rotten apple
All covered in fungus.
Darkness reminds me of scary films
That always make me jump.
Darkness feels like things that are dead
Rotting under the big grey stones.
Darkness tastes like rotten bread
All covered in green and grey fungus.
Darkness looks like Death coming to get you.

Richard McNeil (9)
Fencedyke Primary School, Bourtreehill

Happiness

Happiness smells like fresh grass,
Newly cut,
Happiness smells like sweet honey,
Just been made from bees,
Happiness tastes like smooth creamy chocolate,
Melting on a hot summer's day,
Happiness tastes like sweet sugar,
Dissolving in my coffee,
Happiness feels like soft sand,
Running through my fingertips,
Happiness feels like bouncy beds,
Going up and down,
Happiness sounds like the gentle breeze,
Flowing through the air,
Happiness sounds like gentle waves,
Sailing across the sea,
Happiness looks like colourful butterflies,
Fluttering through the sky,
Happiness looks like stripy bees,
Buzzing into all the flowers,
Happiness reminds me of family times,
When we go on a holiday,
Happiness reminds me of happy times,
Like when we had a family barbecue.
    I love being happy.

Jenifer Russell (9)
Fencedyke Primary School, Bourtreehill

Environment

I see . . . the poachers hunting the animals.

I hear . . . the sound of shredders shredding the trees.

I taste . . . the taste of burning trees turning to ash.

I touch . . . the wet burnt bark on the muddy ground.

I smell . . . the smell of petrol and diesel in the air.

Jordon Tennant (10)
Fencedyke Primary School, Bourtreehill

My Feelings

Listen to the leaves on the tree swaying from side to side.
The leaves falling on the muddy ground all dirty and wet.

Hear the ground rumbling louder and louder as children run.
They are coming near me, they're pulling my bark off
Aargh, aargh! That's sore.
Now they're pulling and trying to break my twigs.
Oh no they've broken one, now they are hitting me with it.

I'm starting to sway, trying to make the leaves fall off,
Falling on their hair all wet and slimy.
There's more rumbling, the children run away leaving the stick
On the ground.
Oh no there's a big lorry, *help me don't cut me.*
I've already had my bark pulled off me and a twig pulled off.
There's a chainsaw
Zzzzzzzzzzzz. Aargh! Zzzzzzzzz.

Kerrie Duff (10)
Fencedyke Primary School, Bourtreehill

Environment

Lots of animals falling to the ground,
Poachers and hunters trying to get them,
Trees falling onto animals, animal homes
Are burning, the animals are petrified.

Animals getting shot, sounds of animals running away,
The ground is shaking and the animals are scared,
The little animals' hearts are beating fast.

Leaves burning down to the bottom of the ground,
Smoke from the guns, lots of fear in my mouth.

The muddy ground with a footprint in it,
My animal friend seeing if it is dead,
The wet bark of the tree melting.

Fumes, diesel and petrol making pollution,
Lots of gun smoke, the animals homes are destroyed.

Daniel McNeil (10)
Fencedyke Primary School, Bourtreehill

Two Sides Of My Forest

One side of my forest
Is very green and alive,
Anyone could live there
Without it being a nightmare,
The other side of my forest
People don't really care,
Come on I'm a tree
Don't you feel it for me?
Is what we all say in our mind?
I wish woodcutters would be more kind,
I wish they could feel what we feel every day,
If only they'd listen to what we've got to say,
As if we're a punchbag, something to hate,
We're not going to stay alive at this rate.
> *Help! Bang! Crash!*

Shannon Bowie (10)
Fencedyke Primary School, Bourtreehill

Happiness

Happiness sounds like birds singing,
When they chirp sweetly.
Happiness tastes sweet and fizzy,
When it touches your mouth.
Happiness smells like melted chocolate,
When it drips down your lips.
Happiness feels like a fluffy pillow,
When I cuddle into it every night.
Happiness looks like a summer sun,
When it shines in the summer.
Happiness reminds me of fun,
When I play with my family.

Chelsie Watson (9)
Fencedyke Primary School, Bourtreehill

Environment

I see . . . the poachers coming towards me,
But as they come they are cutting down the trees and
Shooting my poor animal friends with their horrible weapons.

I hear . . . the rumbling on the ground as the big dangerous lorry
Comes towards me chopping down the trees and ruining our wildlife.

I taste . . . the ruined soggy leaves as they flop off the falling trees
And guess what else I can taste?
It is the gun smoke, the poachers are getting closer.

I touch . . . the poor trees,
They have been knocked down by the bad, nasty, horrible poachers.

I smell . . . the gun smoke of the poachers coming close
And I smell the blood of my poor animal friends
Because they have just been shot.

Oh no! What has happened?

Elizabeth Gray (10)
Fencedyke Primary School, Bourtreehill

The Weather

On Monday it was rain
All day it put me in a lot of pain
On Tuesday it was hail and gale
It made my face go very pale
On Wednesday it was snow and blow
You could almost hear Santa say, 'Ho, ho, ho.'

On Thursday it was thunder and lightning
The sky was very much brightening
On Friday the sky was bright
But the sky was not a delight.
On Saturday it was sunny
The week was very, very funny.

Peter Fulton (10)
Fencedyke Primary School, Bourtreehill

Poor Panda

I see the poachers stamping through
The forest (my home) coming to get me
And other things that I know and love.

I hear their footsteps stamping in the
Wet mud with their huge boots stamping
On sticks and leaves.

I taste the bamboo sticks that I love,
Thinking that some day if people don't
Leave me alone it will all be gone, maybe
Even me.

I touch the muddy ground with my
Paws as I try to get away from the
Horrible people.
Oh wait, they have me surrounded.

I smell the smoke of the gun which
They are trying to shoot me with.
Oh wait, I feel weird, what's happening to me?

Kimberly McLaughlin (11)
Fencedyke Primary School, Bourtreehill

Help, I'm Endangered

I see poachers and hunters everywhere

I hear gunshots in the distance

I taste the fear in my mouth hoping it's not my family

I touch my family as they lie on the muddy ground

I smell the smell of gun smoke as I run and run
Through the big, battered, bare, bony branches
To the remains of my home.

Who am I?
I am Tiger.

Nica Burns (10)
Fencedyke Primary School, Bourtreehill

Shaken

In the morning sunshine I wait for my friends
To awake . . .
When I turn to get a nut I see a poacher
Running towards me,
I start to run as fast as lightning!
I feel the ground shaking
As he gets
Closer and closer to me . . .
I see a tall tree and jump
I start to climb
I get to the highest branch
But I cannot see the poacher!
I can only hear his footsteps
I can hear a fire!
I start to see the smoke going into the sky.
I can feel the trucks getting closer
To destroy
My home
And me.

Julie Davidson (10)
Fencedyke Primary School, Bourtreehill

Wind

I feel the wind but can never hold it
I see it working but hurting the environment
I wonder what the wind really is and how it blows
But never glows
Where does it go when the summer comes?
I want to know, I want to know
In the summer a nice breeze is pleasant
But in winter and cold times a strong wind can blow anyone over.

It harms not just the environment,
But it hurts and maybe even kills the innocent people
Of the world and disturbs the lives of the lucky ones
That have still got their lives to live.

Rachel To (11)
Fencedyke Primary School, Bourtreehill

Environment

I see the poachers heading towards the beautiful trees
In the large green forest which is soon going to be nothing.
I see all the animals and birds running towards me
So I decide to run too.

I smell the gunshot that shoots right through all my animal friends
That it sees or gets to.
I also smell the appalling smell of the oily petrol coming out of the
Colossal lorries, diggers and trucks that are going to cut down
Our wonderful trees.

I hear the gunshots in the distance which is a horrible noise
Of a hunting gun coming closer and closer and closer.
I hear the ground shaking noisily which means that the lorries are
Coming towards me, so I'd better run very fast to get out of here!

I touch the muddy, wet ground when I fall trying to run away
But I manage to get up quickly.
I touch the wet running sap coming out of the tree, how sad.

I taste the fiery, leafy taste which isn't very nice.
I also taste the foggy smell in the air.

Stop cutting down trees!

Rachael Allan (11)
Fencedyke Primary School, Bourtreehill

Environment

I see poachers coming for me, what are they going to do to me?
Don't put me in a cage.
I hear . . . the sound of the frightening gunshot
I taste . . . the bamboo from some leftover trees
I touch . . . the skin of the other dead animals
I smell . . . the burning fire.

Scott Baillie (10)
Fencedyke Primary School, Bourtreehill

Run!

I see . . . hunters coming towards me,
Should I run or should I stay still?
Oh the hunters are coming.
I can see the ground shaking, the grass being stamped on.
He's coming, he's coming, he's coming, he's gone.
I'm safe, I must go home now to see if my darling wife
And cubs are still here in this world.

I hear . . . branches falling to the ground, leaves scattering
Across the ground.
The hunters are walking towards the very last dodo,
What should we do?
Bang! Our dear friend the dodo is gone.
I never thought fast enough.

I smell . . . the blood of the dodo,
The dirt of the hunter's shoes
The lovely fresh water,
I need a drink and so does my family.

I touch . . . the cold water,
The burning leaves,
The damp trees and my family's warmness.
The rain falling on my paws.

Kirsty Hart (11)
Fencedyke Primary School, Bourtreehill

Environment

I see big black smoke past the burning trees.
I hear the gunshots flying through the air, exploding.
I taste the burnt grass, it is dried out.
I touch my animal friend to see if he is alive.
I smell fumes from the gun smoke.

Dale Brown (11)
Fencedyke Primary School, Bourtreehill

Frightened!

Poachers and hunters coming with their bow and arrows,
The arrow is coming nearer and nearer,
It is pointing at my face.

The guns shooting in the distance,
I quickly hide, the ground is shaking because the gunshot is so loud,
The branches fall off the trees and onto the ground.

Smoke, big, black and grey smoke in the air,
I can taste the fear in my mouth.

My heart it is thumping, it feels as if it has come up to my throat,
I shiver with fear as I touch the remains of my home.

Petrol and diesel fumes which go up my nose,
It smells horrible, I hide in a big bundle of leaves.

Melissa Todd (11)
Fencedyke Primary School, Bourtreehill

The Weather

On Monday the wind blew strong,
I sat in the house all day long.
On Tuesday the snow was calm,
The children went out to play with their prams.
On Wednesday there was outbreaks of rain,
The children fell down with pain again.
On Thursday the rain went away
Everyone shouted, 'Hip, hip, hooray.'
On Friday school is over at last
Let's run home very fast.
On Saturday the sun shines with glee
Everyone shouts, 'Yippee!'

Sheridan Russell (10)
Fencedyke Primary School, Bourtreehill

Environment

I see . . . hunters coming into the forest to kill me for my skin
And lumberjacks cutting down trees before I die.
They're going to kill me as soon as they see me!
I see my mother and father getting shot on the spot.
I must get help from the pride to defend our home from these giants
Oh no! They're almost here, I've got to run away from here!
OK, I've got to run. What's that?
I must run like the wind and cover my tracks.
The hunters will not see me when I hide in the grass.

I hear . . . lumberjacks coming to destroy this forest
And everything and every one of my family and me.
I hear lorries coming closer and closer.
The only way to save myself is to leave everyone else behind.
I hear gunshots in the distance and a hunter shouting
'Timberrrrrr!'

I smell . . . a person . . . a man coming . . .
I smell the smoke of his gun.
All I can hope for is a scent . . . a whiff of an animal.
I do not think that I will be able to last the rest, the rest of the day.

Jaspreet Singh (11)
Fencedyke Primary School, Bourtreehill

Sunny Weather

Sunny weather all around
Sunny weather up and down
Sunny weather every day,
Sunny weather on Christmas Day.
Sandals on wherever you go
And then the sun will shine on your toe.
T-shirts on, skirts on, children playing about
The Earth goes round, the day goes on
And I hope the sun will stay!

Tamara McCartney (10)
Fencedyke Primary School, Bourtreehill

Poverty

I see . . . poor miserable children sitting on the cold, damp, mucky
ground with nothing but their own hope.

I hear . . . children shouting out for help.

I taste . . . the rain hitting off their cold faces.

I touch . . . the penny as it is being put in the big round jar.

I smell . . . the fresh baked bread as it is taken out of the van into the
bakery.

Toni McGookin (10)
Fencedyke Primary School, Bourtreehill

In My Summer Garden

I see children and a barbecue and a paddling pool.

I can hear children playing and sausages sizzling
And a barbecue cooking dinner.

I can smell burgers and fresh grass in the breeze and roses.

I can feel the grass under my feet, the warmness rising up
And flowers.

I can taste chocolate ice cream and hot burgers and lovely chips.

George Lawson (8)
Fencedyke Primary School, Bourtreehill

In My Summer Garden

I can see a bird, trampoline and a barbecue.
I can hear birds tweeting, barbecues sizzling and the wind.
I can smell the barbecue, flowers and the grass.
I can feel the grass on my bare feet, the trampoline and the soil.
I can taste burgers, sausages and cola.

Arran Watt (7)
Fencedyke Primary School, Bourtreehill

Environment

Poachers are hunting me, firing guns at me
I see my friends getting shot.
I hear my friends' ferocious roar as they roar in pain.
I taste the thick black smoke where the poachers have lit
A raging fire.
I touch my friend as he lies in pain.
I touch my friend's blood as I walk across the burnt crispy leaves.
I smell the black smoky fire.
At the end of the day I am really sad and scared
As my friends are all hurt and I don't have a home.
I fear this will happen again.

Alexander Taylor (10)
Fencedyke Primary School, Bourtreehill

Poverty

P overty kills mums, dads, brothers, sisters and even babies.
O verall death a minute too many for any country.
V ery bad, something has to be done now.
E ven babies die because of poverty
R aiding through bins looking for food
T oo many people dying -
It is shocking
Y ou can do something!

Declan Hunter (11)
Fencedyke Primary School, Bourtreehill

In My Summer Garden

I can see a swimming pool, chute and swings.
I can hear a bird, children shooting and dogs.
I can smell grass, dog fur and flowers.
I can feel a path, rocks and a gate.
I can taste barbecue, Coke and lemonade.

Jamie Wilson (7)
Fencedyke Primary School, Bourtreehill

The Journey Of Being A Tree

I see children playing hide-and-seek, then . . .
Oh no the woodcutters,
They are coming towards me,
They'll bring out an axe
Then chop me down.
I'm scared of them,
Their big black boots
Crunching the leaves.
Chop! Chop!

I feel sore on the bark of my tree,
But they don't care,
They don't even know
I have feelings.
Five men pick me up
And put me on a truck,
I look to the children,
Staring at my stump and me,
All the sap leaking,
I just look away and shudder.
They've taken me to a paper factory.
Now I'm paper
And the only thing
I see
Is you
Reading
This poem.

Jenn Matthews (10)
Fencedyke Primary School, Bourtreehill

Help!

I feel so peaceful in my lovely home . . .
Nothing could possibly go wrong . . .
Wait a minute!
What's that rumbly sound?
Down there!
A man!
Cutting down my tree!
Quick
I must jump into another tree!

Oh no!
This whole forest is being destroyed,
I can see
The huge, colossal lorries in the distance,
There's five of them!
My heart is in my throat . . .
I can only hear it thumping away.
I must get out of here!
I can hear my family's scampering feet as they desperately
Try to reach the nearby field!
I must join them!

I'm standing here . . .
Watching my home being destroyed.
The machines are going away.
Slowly I walk back
To what was my lovely home.
What shall we do now?

We need help!

Rebecca Johnston (10)
Fencedyke Primary School, Bourtreehill

Trampoline

Big and bouncy
Jumping, doing flips
Black, round
Safety net
Catches you if you fall
Always fun
Playing with your friends
Falling down, have a rest,
It's the best and in the
End it's cool.

Elliott Skeoch (7)
Fencedyke Primary School, Bourtreehill

Teddy

Brown soft fur
Furry round ears
Soft black nose
Red hard eyes
Fat body
Dark brown paws.

Abbie Laing (7)
Fencedyke Primary School, Bourtreehill

My Teddy

Big soft ears
Soft cuddly tummy
Big fat head
Small blue eyes
Big happy smile.

Liam Fitzsimmons (7)
Fencedyke Primary School, Bourtreehill

In My Summer Garden

I can see the sky,
I can see a trampoline,
I see children.

I can hear my brother playing in the pool,
I can hear lots of noise,
I can hear people outside.

I can smell barbecue,
I can smell the air-freshener,
I can smell a lovely smell.

I can feel grass,
I can feel plants,
I can feel petals.

I can taste toasties,
I can taste meat,
I can taste ice cream.

Luke McNeil (7)
Fencedyke Primary School, Bourtreehill

In My Summer Garden

I can see children playing on a trampoline.
I see the sea.
I can see my car.

I can hear a bird tweeting,
I can hear children playing,
And I can hear a barbecue.

I can smell a barbecue, I can smell the sea.

I can taste a burger, I can taste juice,
I can taste the barbecue.

Scott McKie (7)
Fencedyke Primary School, Bourtreehill

Environment

I see poachers chasing a furry black and white panda
It tries to hide in the snow on the mountain
And the loving panda hides its tiny little baby panda.
The poachers are pointing their guns at the pandas
And they are crying for help.

I hear *bang! Bang! Bang!*
People are shouting at the poachers.
Saying, 'Stop that you poachers!'
I hear the lorries driving away, far, far away.

I taste the fear of the dead pandas.

I smell the dead pandas' wet blood running past like a small lake.

I touch the bright red blood
Then I touch the dead pandas' fur.

Louise Morrison (10)
Fencedyke Primary School, Bourtreehill

In My Summer Garden

I can see children on the trampoline,
Gran in the swimming pool
And a barbecue.

I can hear children playing,
Hose water and the wind.

I can smell barbecue smoke, the flowers
And the grass.

I can feel my sunbed, my feet in the water,
Silky flowers.

I can taste Coca-Cola, sausage roll and burgers.

Callum Reilly (7)
Fencedyke Primary School, Bourtreehill

In My Summer Garden

I can see children playing games, sparklers in the air and flowers.

I can hear children talking, a barbecue and bees buzzing.

I can smell smoke, the flowers and someone cooking.

I can feel the grass, the silky flowers and water on my feet.

I can taste the sausages I am about to eat,
The Coca-Cola I'm about to drink
And the nice burger I'm about to eat.

Malcolm West (7)
Fencedyke Primary School, Bourtreehill

In My Summer Garden

I can see a paddling pool, a hut and a trampoline.

I can hear children, birds and my mum.

I can smell barbecues, sausages and the flowers.

I can feel the water splashing and the sunbed
And the sun shining on my face.

I can taste the ice cream, ice poles and
A lollipop.

Ross Skivington (7)
Fencedyke Primary School, Bourtreehill

In My Summer Garden

I can see a trampoline, a barbecue and some children.
I can hear birds singing, people in a paddling pool
and people running.
I can smell a barbecue, a burger and a hot dog.
I can feel water, grass and petals.
I can taste ice cream, burgers and sausages.

Leon Hendry (7)
Fencedyke Primary School, Bourtreehill

In My Summer Garden

I can see the sky, the sun and the clouds.

I can hear my brother splashing in the pool,
My mum saying stop splashing,
And my dad talking to my nanna and papa.

I can smell a barbecue, the flowers and the sun cream
On my brother.

I can taste a drink my mum gives me,
Ice cream my dad gives me
And a kiss my dad gives me.

Ashley Wilson (7)
Fencedyke Primary School, Bourtreehill

In My Summer Garden

I can see a barbecue, children and a trampoline.
I can hear whistling, birds tweeting and talking.
I can smell sausages, burgers and hot dogs.
I can feel my toes, clothes and grass.
I can taste chips, drinks and fruit.

Robbie Taylor (7)
Fencedyke Primary School, Bourtreehill

In My Summer Garden

I can see a trampoline, a slide and a barbecue.
I can hear a band, children and people shouting.
I can smell a barbecue, flowers and the sea.
I can feel the grass, the heat and the trees.
I can taste a sausage, a burger and an ice cream.

Christopher Gunn (7)
Fencedyke Primary School, Bourtreehill

In My Summer Garden

I can see a picnic, bouncy castle and a sandpit.

I can hear children shouting, the waves crashing
Against the rocks and bees humming.

I can smell barbecues, smoke and grass.

I can feel the heat on my skin,
The grass rubbing against my feet and petals of flowers.

I can taste burgers, Coca-Cola and buns.

Haven-Lee Walker (7)
Fencedyke Primary School, Bourtreehill

In My Summer Garden

I can see a pool, children playing and my mum and dad.

I can hear the birds, the grass and the water from the hose.

I can smell the barbecue, the flowers and the smoke from the
barbecue.

I can feel the water, my dog and the grass.

I can taste fruit salad, ice poles and fruit.

Leah Hamilton (7)
Fencedyke Primary School, Bourtreehill

In My Summer Garden

I can see children playing, Granny in the pool
And lots of flowers.

I can hear birds tweeting, children talking and feet moving.

I can smell barbecues, flowers and cut grass.

I can feel grass, smooth petals and the hot ground from the sun.

I can taste burgers, hot dogs and bacon.

Toni Morgan (8)
Fencedyke Primary School, Bourtreehill

In My Summer Garden

I can see the flowers getting blown in the wind,
I can see children playing,
I can see people coming back from the shop.

I can hear the birds singing,
I can hear children shouting and screaming,
I can hear sizzling from the barbecue.

I can smell the smoke from the barbecue,
I can smell the sweet lovely flowers,
I can smell the smoke from the cars that are going by.

I can feel the grass tickling my feet,
I can feel the hotness on my skin,
I can feel flowers touching my hand.

I can taste the ice cream that my dad has brought for me,
I can taste the fizzy cola that my mum made,
I can taste oranges that my nan has bought for me.

Ellie McTear (7)
Fencedyke Primary School, Bourtreehill

A Week Of Blustery Weather

On Monday blustery rains pour and
The heavy winds roar and roar.

On Tuesday there is patchy mist and
Blustery wind blows against my wrist.

Wednesday gales bash against the trees
And heavy snow blows against our knees.

On Thursday persistent rain
And heavy snow blows again.

Friday clears but mist will lift
And we will have a dry day, hooray.

Saturday, sun's come out finally and
Blue skies arrive again.

Callum Drysdale (10)
Fencedyke Primary School, Bourtreehill

In My Summer Garden

I can see the slide, the paddling pool
And the trampoline.

I can smell a barbecue, the sea and the flowers.

I can hear children playing, a pan sizzling
And people talking.

I can feel the grass, the flowers and the mud.

I can taste an ice lolly, a sausage roll
And a sour lemon.

Natasha Duncan (7)
Fencedyke Primary School, Bourtreehill

In My Summer Garden

I can see a trampoline, a barbecue and children playing.

I can hear a balloon going bang,
A motorbike and a ball getting bounced.

I can smell sausages cooking,
A lovely cake and lots of flowers.

I can feel petals, the hard ground and lots of grass.

I can taste marshmallows, a nice cold glass of lemonade
And a sugary chocolate bun.

Carly McGowan (7)
Fencedyke Primary School, Bourtreehill

In My Summer Garden

I can see children, a pool and a chute.
I can hear laughter, people and a child playing.
I can smell flowers, food and a barbecue.
I can feel grass, petals and plants.
I can taste sandwiches, meat and an ice pole.

Shannon Flynn (7)
Fencedyke Primary School, Bourtreehill

And Here Is The Weather

On Monday the wind blew through our streets,
Everyone's things were certainly not neat.

On Tuesday the day was dull,
Not good weather when we're supposed to be in May.

On Wednesday there will be persistent rain,
No one will get to play their games again.

On Thursday, outbreaks of rain,
This is really starting to become a pain.

On Friday hundreds of patchy clouds,
Everyone is complaining and shouting really loud.

On Saturday sunny spells as far as I can see,
This day is going to be all about me.

Megan Donnelly (10)
Fencedyke Primary School, Bourtreehill

The Miserable Week

On Monday there is heavy rain
No more games of tig again.
On Tuesday it is very cloudy
In the classroom it is rowdy.
On Wednesday it is rainy and snowy
All the week you will see Zoe.
On Thursday it is very cold
And it makes me very bored.
On Friday the clouds are out
Oh no we can't go out.
Here we are Saturday today
Great weather and we can go out, hooray!

Zoe Jardine (10)
Fencedyke Primary School, Bourtreehill

A Week Of Lost Summer Sun

Monday has storms and gale,
All you can hear is the wind moan and wail.

On Tuesday everyone hides under
The tables because there is loud, loud thunder.

Wednesday's weather's a little better,
But I think it's a wee bit wetter.

Thursday's rain fell heavily down,
I don't like bad weather, it makes me frown.

Friday's weather's a lot, lot worse,
Maybe our school has a bad weather curse.

On Saturday there's a clear blue sky,
But sometimes I wonder . . . why?

Lorin Kirk (11)
Fencedyke Primary School, Bourtreehill

A Week Of Horrible Weather

On Monday the rain came pouring down,
Λ dull morning with low cloud.
On Tuesday the rain was still continuing
And all the children were so bored.
On Wednesday all I could hear was
Thunder and lightning, I was so angry.
On Thursday it was gale force winds,
I thought it was never going to end.
On Friday the sky was very dull,
I could barely see anything, uh.
On Saturday I woke up, it was all gone, *hooray!*

Emma Strachan (11)
Fencedyke Primary School, Bourtreehill

Senses

I like the look of sunshine
Shining on the sea.
I like the feel of toothpaste
Squashy as can be.
I like the smell of church bells
Very grand indeed.
I like the taste of roses
Refreshing my mouth.
I like the sound of mountains
Roaring very loudly.

Megan Shearer (8)
Fishermoss Primary School, Portlethen

I Like My Senses

I like the feel of toothpaste,
Squishing through my teeth,
I like the look of sunshine
Beating on my face
I like the sound of church bells
Singing in my ear
I like the smell of mountains
Echoing everywhere
I like the taste of roses
Growing every year.

Charlotte Torrance (8)
Fishermoss Primary School, Portlethen

I Like Senses

I like the feel of toothpaste
Squishing through my fingers.
I like the sound of roses
Blowing in the wind.
I like the taste of sunshine
Shining on my face.
I like the look of church bells
Ringing from side to side.
I like the smell of mountains
Refreshing the air.

Kirsty Duncan (8)
Fishermoss Primary School, Portlethen

Skating

I was skating in da skatepark, yeah,
Flippin' on my board
Hit da ramps, 360 flip right through the air I soared
My friends showed up a bit later
They all 'ad brilliant boards
'Dat's da way I like it,' they said
An' I was just ignored.

They said I was stupid but,
Dat time they were ignored
I went 'ome dat minute
Cos I was gettin' bored
But they just kept on trickin'
Until their mummies called
'Time for bed all you lot
Your supper's gettin' cold.'

Keiran De La Mare (9)
Golfhill Primary School, Airdrie

My Real Love

My real love goes to the baths on Saturdays
I really wish I could go with her.

But I can't because I go to football training
And sometimes it feels like it's raining

I really want to know her name
I don't think I ever will

And when I went to school
I was lucky because I got to speak with her
In private behind a corner

She asked me, 'What are you doing?'
I said, 'I want to know your name.'

She said, 'My name is Gillian. What's yours?'
'Calum,' I said. 'Don't tell anyone this but I love you.'
She looked at me and blushed
'Well I do too,' she said, and we held hands.

Calum Paterson (8)
Golfhill Primary School, Airdrie

Lonely

No one likes being lonely
It makes people feel sad
Some people want company
Some people just go mad.

Sometimes when I am lonely
I'll go upstairs and act funny
Wanting some company
Like anyone would when they are lonely.

Jack Black (8)
Golfhill Primary School, Airdrie

Which Pet Should I Get?

Should I get a crocodile, green and scaly
With its great big jaws, snap, snap, snap?

Or a rabbit cute and hairy,
And gnaws on a carrot all day long?

What about a parrot shouting in my ear
But its lovely colours brightening up my day?

Or even a dragon of which have a fear
And he breathes out fire to toast marshmallows?

Or a monkey who scratches his head
And eats bananas but not the skins?

What about a spider crawling up my leg
Who bites me with his sharp, sharp fangs?

I know a squirrel climbing up the trees
And finding lots of nuts for lunch and dinner.

Or a horse galloping in the breeze
And what about his long tail and mane?

An elephant with a rider on his back
And his big feet, stomp, stomp, stomp!

Or a seal who swims in a pack
And eats lots of fish, yum, yum, yum!

Hmmm what about a dodo who doesn't fly
But he was extinct years ago?

I know, a dog that can jump up high,
And loves bones, yum, yum, yum!

What about a pig who eats all day
And rolls in the mud and gets messy?

Or a dolphin that likes to play
And jumps up high, really high?

I know my favourite, the cat,
I think I will get one for me!

Kirsty Irvine (10)
Kinnoull Primary School, Perth

Dragons

A dragon with its fiery breath,
Breathing the hot air,
Dragons ensure a painful death,
Of that I can be sure.

A dragon with its tiny scales,
Green and red with gore,
Dragons ensure a painful death,
Of that I can be sure.

A dragon with its huge long tail,
Like an arrow with a point,
Dragons ensure a painful death,
Of that I can be sure.

A dragon swimming in hot lava,
Takes the heat without a palaver,
Dragons ensure a painful death,
Of that I can be sure.

A dragon guarding the little princess,
Her rags were supposed to be a white dress,
Dragons ensure a painful death,
Of that I can be sure.

Holly Buchanan (10)
Kinnoull Primary School, Perth

Elves

Elves are very small creatures,
They have tiny features,
Some are moss elves,
Some like leaves,
Even some dwell in the trees!

The ruler of the elves was called Falleta,
Got a cold and didn't get better.
So they are seeking a new king,
One that is fun and might dance and sing!

Fairies and elves are good friends,
The parties with each other never ends,
Only sometimes they invite the dwarves,
Because they steal afterwards,
Because they love gold,
More than a story told,
So they are sometimes forbidden from the parties!

Now if you see an elf about,
Please don't step on him,
Because that is a *big* sin!

My story is told,
I have let it unfold,
As I've said the dwarves would prefer gold!

Sylvie Kay (11)
Kinnoull Primary School, Perth

Meeting The Queen

I met the Queen a year ago,
It was most important to me, so
I got out my hat and my flowery dress,
And tried to make sure my hair wasn't a mess!
I got into the car and drove out and away,
And before long I was on the motorway.
After (it seemed) years of driving,
I could see signposts for London and the weather was thriving.
I was soon sitting in a long traffic jam,
And everything was ever so calm.
All the cars soon pulled away,
I was at the palace, hip, hip, hooray!
A palace guard came and took my arm,
It was obvious he would do me no harm.
I wiped my feet on the 'Welcome' doormat
And saw an armchair in which I sat.
After a moment I heard a click-clack,
Of posh shoes which were actually black.
And then the Queen entered, I at once stood and bowed,
She smiled at me in a way that looked proud.
She beckoned to her guard to bring me some tea,
While she herself had a frothy coffee.
Then she said, 'Can I ask you a question?'
I answered, 'Yes.'
She took a deep breath, 'Why, is there egg on your dress?'

Ciara Hayes (11)
Kinnoull Primary School, Perth

Stars

Years and years ago, through the night,
Dark was the sky and the stars were bright,
I looked up to the stars, I watched and lay,
But when it was morning they faded away.

Now the air is black with smoke,
And the sky is wrapped up in a brown-grey cloak.
We are the culprits of this crime,
If I could, then up to the heavens I'd climb

And brush away the smoke, vanish it forever,
So that the Earth and the sky could be together,
Well somebody tell me when, when, *when,*
Will we ever see the stars again?

Catriona Anderson (10)
Kinnoull Primary School, Perth

It's Good To Be Different

It's good to be different!
It's very good to be different!
If we were not different
We would all be the same
And have the same
Mother and the same father,
We would be the same colour,
We would like the same people,
You would not know who's who,
Even if it was you!
So just remember that
It's good to be different
It's very good to be different!

Emili Harris (9)
Ladybank Primary School, Ladybank

Anger

Anger drives me crazy!
Anger drives me mad!
I'm a kettle,
I screech and squeal and shake!
Anger drives me crazy!

Anger drives me crazy!
Anger drives me mad!
I am a dictionary
Of words I can't write down,
They're too rude!

Anger drives me crazy!
Anger drives me mad!
I'm a wild animal on the rampage,
I kick, shout and stomp!

Anger drives me crazy!
Anger drives me mad!
I'm a wasp,
I sting everyone in sight,
Then suddenly I take flight!

Anger drives me crazy!
Anger drives me mad!
I'm a poisonous gas!
I fill rooms
And hiss under doors!

Anger drives me crazy!

Eilidh Lewis (9)
Ladybank Primary School, Ladybank

Racism

Racism doesn't have a smell
but it is rotten.

Racism doesn't have a taste
but it's sickening.

Racism doesn't have a look
but it seems so cruel.

Racism doesn't have a sound
but it hurts my ear.

Racism doesn't have a feel
but it's prickly.

So I hope now you know
that it's cold to be racist
not cool.

Katie Coull (10)
Ladybank Primary School, Ladybank

Racism!

Racism does not smell
But in a way it does.
Even if they just call us a
Name it still hurts us.

Racism is not a game,
It's good that we're not the same.
Why do some people think it's fun?
I'd rather sit in the sun.

Racism is a horrible thing,
It's all about the colour of your skin.
Some people are a different colour
But inside we're the same as each other.

Siobhan Laing (9)
Ladybank Primary School, Ladybank

Volcanic Eruption

If I am angry, don't come near me
Because I'll blow
There will be bits of me everywhere
And it won't be a pretty sight
You might get a fright
But no one can feel the pain I'm going through but me.
The pain is unreal
It is like fire burning my skin
And it does not look nice
It is like I have sliced my skin open
Ouch, it is so, so painful
Fire is burning
And tearing
And slicing
My skin
Ouch,
It is sore.

Steven Anderson (10)
Ladybank Primary School, Ladybank

Fear

I may look like a strong man,
Fearless and all,
But inside I'm full of fear
Because I'm really scared of bullies and heights.

People think I'm really unkind and nasty,
I really don't like that
Because I'm nice and care for others.

My worst fear is monsters at night,
I cuddle my teddy bear
And hope that they won't clamber out of my closet.

I may look like a strong man,
Fearless and all,
But inside I'm full of fear.

Cameron Brown (9)
Ladybank Primary School, Ladybank

Anger

When I'm angry I am like a wasp
Buzzing and buzzing until you come close
Then I . . .
. . . *Sting you!*

Anger makes me tight
Like an elastic band
Stretching and pulling
Until I . . .
. . . Snap and ping you!

When I'm angry my eyes pop out like corks
Popping out of wine bottles!

Anger makes me hold my teeth together
Like they're going to . . .
. . . Snap!

Bethany Smith (9)
Ladybank Primary School, Ladybank

An Evil Cactus

The evil cactus ate a lot of owls
with a flickering liquorice tongue.
The evil cactus ate a lot of owls
with a deadly flickering liquorice tongue
that sticks out at them.
He looks like a spike bomb
with a sharp, pointy head.
He looks like a spike bomb
with a huge, sharp, pointy head
that looks like an arrow.

Sean Brown (11)
Ladybank Primary School, Ladybank

Racism

It would not be very good
If we had the same name
It would not be very good
If we were all the same
None of us are the same
And racism is lame
That is why some of us
Wear racism bands
We wear them on our wrists
We don't hold them in our hands.

We get called names
Because of our skin
We'd get called names
If we were all thin
Racism stinks, it really, really does
It hurts you, it hurts all of us.

Christopher Royle (9)
Ladybank Primary School, Ladybank

The Children Eater

The monster lives in a glowing, gungy, deep, dark cave,
It lives all alone and is so, so greedy.
The children think he's frightening, and he is he's terrifying,
But the monster is scared of their mums and dads!

He eats children but he does not like the way they look,
So he closes his eyes and gobbles them up.
Quickly before their mums and dads catch him.

He looks terrible, he has big ears, wiggly legs and smelly clothes,
He's got sharp teeth, a big greedy grin, goggly eyes and a pointy
                                                      nose.
He growls and grunts every single day.

Caitlin Self (10)
Ladybank Primary School, Ladybank

Anger

I'm a red-hot volcano
If people get close I will burn them to ashes
My fire is the hottest thing on the planet
My fists are like rocks
My teeth are sealed tight
My eyes have popped
All because the Sellotape wouldn't come off my birthday present!

Aaron Shand (9)
Ladybank Primary School, Ladybank

Anger

When I'm angry I feel fizzy,
I feel hot,
I want to erupt
Like a red-hot volcano.
My head gets tighter and tighter and tighter until it bursts!
If people come near me
I sting them like a bee.
If people come near me
I burn them.

Alasdair Robertson (9)
Ladybank Primary School, Ladybank

Anger

When I'm angry I go really mad
And then I go in my room
And I stay there.

I watch my television
And when it's finished
I go back through
And say sorry.

Kelly Martin (12)
Ladybank Primary School, Ladybank

The Violent Teacher

He does not have feet
All that he has are after burners
He always wears an indigo hat
With a bubble on the top.

He has extremely sharp teeth
He eats cats and rats
He eats skies and pies
He eats schoolchildren.

He lives in dustbins
Covered in tins
He lives in a dump
He looks like a lump in the dump.

Josh Whitelaw (9)
Ladybank Primary School, Ladybank

If The World . . .

If the world was made of paper I would
draw loads of pictures all over the world.
I would draw until it is so beautiful
I would make the world love us
and I would stop the cruel people doing the bad things.
I would let them do anything except destroy the world.
If the houses were made of paper I would decorate them
until everybody loved them to pieces.
If the pets were made of feathers
I would make them have the cleanest claws invented.

Jonathan Simpson (10)
Ladybank Primary School, Ladybank

My Friends

My friends are cool,
My friends are great,
My friends are wonderful people
You could never ever hate.

Our friendship grows
Each and every day,
But the day it blooms best,
Is in the month of May.

They make me feel so special,
In each and every way,
They make me feel like this
Every single day.

When I hear their laughter,
It brightens up my day,
Because that special laughter,
Is one that never goes away.

I see their smiling faces,
Grinning all around,
I could notice them anywhere,
Even in a huge, big crowd.

Our friendship is,
As hard as a rock,
And no one will break it,
Not even a dog.

Amanda Melville (12)
Ladyton Primary School, Bonhill

The Colour Of Friendship

Friendship is colourful
Friendship is nice
Friendship is something you never can hate.
Friendship can grow like a flower.

When you're down your friend will be there to make you
Laugh again.
The footsteps of a friend will make you feel safe and warm.
Friendship makes you feel that you're not alone.

Friendship is colourful
Friendship is nice
Friendship is something you never can hate,
Friendship can grow like a flower.

I can hear the laughter of friends and the wind too,
Friendship can be painful, sometimes
Until you can see the smiles on their faces.

Samantha Davidson (10)
Ladyton Primary School, Bonhill

Summer

Summer, summer, it's so good,
Summer, summer, it puts me in the mood,
For football and basketball, it's so great
It is summer you can never hate.

Summer, summer, it's so fun,
With the bright yellow sun,
The sun also has orange too,
And I wonder if it smells like a shoe.

Summer, summer, it's the best,
It is far greater than the rest,
You can be happy, you can play,
Because it might be sunny every day.

Alexander Dow (11)
Ladyton Primary School, Bonhill

Friendships

Friendship is nice, happy and fun
When I make new friends a flower begins to sprout out and grow,
I hear my friends' footsteps
They make me feel safe and protected
When I see my friends
They put a smile on my face;
Ear to ear.
I feel warm, happy, protected and safe.
I feel like they are guarding me.
My friendship grows and grows.
The flower grows too.
Then suddenly my flower seems to be going down,
Down and down.
I wonder why?
Are we falling apart?
That's when we often move on to make new friends,
And this time let's make my flower grow
And never let it die.

Emma Evans (10)
Ladyton Primary School, Bonhill

My Best Friend Loren

I see her eyes and they shine like the sun,
Her hair is dark and fair but never moves in the air,
My friend is an open heart for me to see,
My friend will let me dance or sing or do anything,
My friend will share because she's fair,
She will help me if I am hurt or if I am in the dirt.

All the things that you will see
Show you why she's right for me!

Shannon McKeown (11)
Ladyton Primary School, Bonhill

My Best Friends

My friendship is like a powerful seed,
That is determined to succeed.

I see all the clouds disappear
When they are very nearly here.

I hear their footsteps on the ground
Then I hear no sudden sound.

I know they are there for me when I'm down
They always act like a silly clown.

There is never anyone in the lead
So that's why we always succeed!

So there are my best friends
And it sends a clear message
On what my friendship is like!

Chloe Beck (11)
Ladyton Primary School, Bonhill

Friends

I have got lots of friends
Although there are three that are the best.
We've had our ups and downs
That we've worked round.
I could never imagine life
Without them around.
Every day our friendship grows and grows,
And we get closer.
We manage to get through the worst
And when we move on to the Academy,
We'll get through it because we can do.

Jacqueline Moir (12)
Ladyton Primary School, Bonhill

My Best Friend Shannon

I can see her brown eyes twinkling at me
She is the best friend that ever could be
If she wasn't my best friend
Then the world could just go and end.

I can hear giggles and laughter
I leave my dinner I'll get it after
Shannon's here
I know she's near
All my problems disappear.

I can feel the sun above me
When I hear that she is coming
We spend all night running free
Then we stop to climb a tree
She is the best friend that ever could be.

Loren McCuish (10)
Ladyton Primary School, Bonhill

Summer

I love summer
It's as if it's just for me
But the things I like most would be:

The brave deer stomping through the lush green fields,
And the farmers facing what the fields may yield.

The busy buzzy fuzzy bees buzzing all about
Collecting pollen in and out.
The twittering birds singing to me
And all the bunny rabbits hopping with glee.

I love summer
It's as if it's just for me
I love summer because of all the fuzzy buzzy bees.

Kayleigh Roberts (11)
Ladyton Primary School, Bonhill

Anger

Anger is as red as a burning fire.
It sounds like waves crashing against the rocks.
It tastes like fiery hot chilli peppers.
It smells like my dinner burning in the kitchen.
It looks like a fierce bull about to charge.
It feels like boiling water burning my arm.
It reminds me to hold onto my temper.

Ellie Scott (10)
Luss Primary School, Luss

Happiness

Happiness is yellow like a giant blazing sun,
It sounds like children laughing on a summer's day,
It tastes like a big bowl of strawberry ice cream,
It smells like a fresh, blooming tulip,
It looks like a big yellow smiley face,
It feels like my mum giving me a hug when I'm upset,
It reminds me of lambs in the fields in spring.

Stephy Woods (10)
Luss Primary School, Luss

Silence

Silence is white like snow in December,
It sounds like the wind on a still winter's day,
It tastes like the coldness of melting ice,
It smells like the coldness of frost,
It looks like a pine tree blanketed in snow,
It feels like the fur on a newborn kitten,
It reminds me of Christmas on a calm, snowy night.

Rhianna Baxter (10)
Luss Primary School, Luss

Hunger

Hunger is black as a black hole in space.
It sounds like a screaming male blackbird.
It tastes like the sourness in my mouth when it's dry.
It smells like a chocolate cake just out of reach.
It looks like a pizza on a table which doesn't exist.
It feels like a rumbling volcano crashing through a village.
It reminds me of an empty room in an empty house.

Sean McPhail (10)
Luss Primary School, Luss

Fun

Fun is orange like a warm summer sun
It sounds like the laughter of my friends running around
It tastes like a hot, steaming chocolate brownie
It smells like a bunch of lavender freshly picked from the riverside
It looks like the night-time stars twinkling in the sky
It feels like an applause at the end of a show
It reminds me of having Christmas dinner with my family.

Alice Rankin (11)
Luss Primary School, Luss

Anger

Anger is scarlet like smouldering coal.
It sounds like a chorus of babies wailing.
It tastes like the bitterness of a friend who won't talk.
It smells like black smoke choking my lungs.
It looks like a blazing fire out of control.
It feels like rough sandpaper scratching my hands.
It reminds me of my brother's insults.

Robbie Anderson (11)
Luss Primary School, Luss

Fun

Fun is yellow like a tropical Caribbean sunset.
It sounds like the calm waves that sweep away the relaxed
fish sunbathing on the golden sand,
It tastes like creamy lemon meringue ice cream that melts on a
summer's day,
It smells like freshly baked apple pie left by the window to cool down,
It looks like a diamond shiny rainbow hanging over me,
It feels like an expensive silk dress waiting to be worn,
It reminds me of all my family and friends!

Hayley Gray (11)
Luss Primary School, Luss

Happiness

Happiness is green like the grass in a lush green meadow.
It sounds like children being entertained by a clown at the circus.
It tastes like sugary, sticky candyfloss.
It smells like a pack of cheese and onion crisps fresh out of the
larder.
It looks like children playing on a water slide.
It feels like the warm water in a swimming pool as you dive in.
It reminds me of when I went skiing.

Hamish Marsh (11)
Luss Primary School, Luss

Take A Look At The World Today, What A Mess

Take a look at the world today,
What a mess.

People starving,
People dying,
People homeless,
People crying.

Look at the world today,
What a mess.

People happy,
People sad,
People joyful,
People mad.

Take a look at the mess today,
What a mess.

People homeless,
In need of food,
People helpless,
Never good.

Take a look at the world today
What a mess . . .

Stacy Thomson (12)
Macduff School, Macduff

Nuclear In Hiroshima

Playing cricket in the park,
With all my friends.
We hear a faint buzzing overhead,
As we look up it comes nearer.

Within minutes the buzzing sound is so loud,
We have to cover our ears,
The thing is above our heads.
It's a plane,
A large, green plane.

A large cylinder drops out of the plane,
And drops to the ground,
The plane speeds away,
The thing falls to the ground,
A bomb.

Boom! goes the bomb,
The heat is unbearable,
A large mushroom shape rises,
Up, up into the sky,
It's coming towards us.

By now the heat is so high my skin is burning,
Everyone is running away,
I hear crashes overhead,
I see buildings collapsing to the ground,
Nuclear.

The bomb fades away,
People are lying on the ground,
Burnt, hurt from the terrible bomb,
Ambulances are rushing everywhere,
If only the bomb hadn't come.

People are dying,
Right there in the street,
I run wishing my family were OK,
I can't find my house for all the rubble,
I ask a policeman if he has heard of them . . .

He gives me the news,
They died when the bomb was dropped,
It was dropped beside their offices,
I stand there waiting for someone to come for me,
No one comes . . .

Leona McKenzie (12)
Macduff School, Macduff

My Dog Suzie

I have a dog called Suzie
She's really cute and fluffy
She really likes her treats
She's not a very big toughie.

She plays out in the garden
She chases a blue ball
She runs so fast all the time
She sometimes trips and falls!

All the time I hear a woof
She makes a mess everywhere
Muddy prints on the carpet
Even on the stairs

But I love her every day
Even when she's a pain
She makes me happy all the time
I'll always remember her name!
Suzie's the *best!*

Amanda Watt (12)
Macduff School, Macduff

All About Me

James Andrew Geddes
Is my name
I live in Macduff
Where I am a pain.

I like to play football
And other games
I also play basketball
But it's not the same.

My dad is called Peter
He is a big eater
My mum is Yvonne
And she's always on the phone.

My favourite food is curry
And sometimes I worry
That I get a sore tummy
Then I eat McFlurry.

My favourite car is Ford
I think they're ace
My brother can play guitar chords
At a certain pace.

That is my poem
All about me
I hope you enjoyed it
We will see.

James Geddes (11)
Macduff School, Macduff

Tsunami

I sat on the sand,
Looking out to sea,
And then the ground shook,
Something is happening to me.

I felt a bit strange,
But I couldn't see,
Everything was quiet,
Something is happening to me.

I saw a small wave,
Far off on the sea,
Getting bigger and faster,
Coming closer to me.

Is it a storm?
It couldn't be,
The sky is still blue,
What's happening to me?

I stood up and ran,
Across the burning sand,
Trying to find some safety,
I hope I can.

I found a safe place,
High up on a cliff,
I saw a monstrous wave,
I stood there scared stiff.

I reached the top,
And crouched down low,
And prayed to God,
For it to go.

Danielle Murdoch (11)
Macduff School, Macduff

A Victorian Winter

(This poem was inspired by the story 'The Little Match Girl')

It's cold in London town
As snowflakes fall from the sky
A chilly breeze blows through the streets
And I begin to cry.

Our house is just a shack
In the corner of the street
With no heating except
A fire to warm our feet.

I live here with my brother
Who is dying from the flu
My mother has gone
I soon shall die too.

Suddenly I hear a gasp
I look round for my brother
He's gone, disappeared!
I weep and weep and shiver.

Then I feel warmth surrounding me
Feathers tickle my shoulder
Then I feel a presence behind me
I take my last deep breath
Then float off to Heaven.

Ellie Wiseman (11)
Macduff School, Macduff

Best Friends

There were three friends,
Who played and played,
The day had to end,
But their friendship still stayed!

They each went home,
And took off their shoes,
They packed away their things,
And went for a snooze!

The morning came,
They each woke up,
They put on their lip gloss,
And walked their pup!

As the day went on,
And it got dark,
Their friendship grew stronger,
In their favourite park!

Debbie Fowlie (12)
Macduff School, Macduff

Tammy And Tasha

Go Tammy, you go,
So keep to the flow,
You are my dog,
You are the best,
So go and keep to the flow.

Here's Tasha my dog,
She is so cool,
When we go to the beach,
She goes mental and sniffs stones,
And goes in the pool.

By night they are so tired,
That a click of the fingers
Sends them to sleep.

Chelsea Barber (12)
Macduff School, Macduff

Awa Up In Outer Space

Fit wid it be like?
Weel
Ken this? I *hate* it 'ere coz there ain't a lot tae dee!
Well it's a richt looking at the bonnie stars and athin but there's
An awfa, *mingin* smell.
It's like fooshty cheese and a heap o' rotten eggs!
But then again . . . it has its gweed pints!
I saw a rocket fleein' past mi!
Michty me ma hairt wiz in ma moo!
I got such a *fleg!*
There aint a lot o' action 'ere bit there are a few funny fowk gan
                                                    aboot.

They're richt tall and skinny
I felt a bit oot o'place coz they're so much different fae me!
They dinna *hae skin!*
They're a' *reeng* and *yalla!*
They look quite slimy . . . yuk!
There's nae a lot o soons oot 'ere . . . well . . .
Except for the soon o' bubblin' lava!
It's like ma *granny biling* a pan o' tattie soup
But *tatti soup* tastes better!
I'm chokin' up and I need some watter ower ma throat!
I wid like to ging to the sun . . . but . . .
I'd sizzle to death - like sausages in a pan!
Ouch! . . . well I better get hame
I'll *tell* you . . .
This hame on Earth his nivver soonded better.

Amber Lorimer (11)
Macduff School, Macduff

Eye Of The Storm

I'm in the eye of the storm,
Nothing is moving, I'm scared.
In the distance, I see something,
Something, I don't know what it is.

It looks like a cone,
Or maybe the shape of a bone.
I don't know what,
But the winds are picking up.

It's lifting up cars and cows,
I'm running but it seems as though I'm not.
I think I'm getting dragged towards it,
I know what it is, it's a *hurricane*.

I looked for Mum, she was gone,
The house was gone too,
I wished it would go away,
When I prayed, I thought it was a dream, but it wasn't.

Louise Mackinnon (11)
Macduff School, Macduff

Jumping Day!

I'm in the stable with my horse,
Today we're doing a jumping course.
I'm going to get him all tacked up,
And hope that we will win the cup.
Bridle, saddle, stirrups too,
And on the hooves four lucky horseshoes.
We're riding out now to the crowd,
They're clapping and cheering me on aloud.
I'm cantering over the jumps so fast,
I hope this moment will always last.
'We've won the cup,' I shout, 'Hooray!'
I can't wait to compete another day.

Emily Coleman (11)
Mill O' Forest Primary School, Stonehaven

My Netball Team!

Such a big hall,
How could you hear a call?
It is such an amazing place,
You should see the players' face.

It helps if you are tall,
So you can catch the winning ball,
In the net,
I'll bet!

Who's the winning team?
Mill O' Forest are the ones who beam,
Come on shake hands,
And smile to the fans.

Caitlyn Cheyne (11)
Mill O' Forest Primary School, Stonehaven

Football Match

Running down the wing so fast,
I beat a man and then I pass
The man receives and takes control
He takes a shot and hits the pole.

The goalie takes a massive kick,
The striker takes a skilful flick,
The right midfield is through on goal,
The shot comes from his very soul.

It flew past him as fast as light,
It was a goal, to the fans' delight,
The whistle's blown, it's the end of the game,
They lose 5-0, the keeper's to blame.

Danny Malcolm (11)
Mill O' Forest Primary School, Stonehaven

The Rally

Starting up engines
The sound is so amazing
Mechanics changing the tyres
It's a sound that inspires

Someone makes the stage clear
The crowd gives a giant cheer
As the car goes over the bumps
As crazy as adrenaline pumps

Someone has to win it all
Second is nothing at all
The winner wins £10,000
The loser gets crushed into the ground.

Daniel Paterson (11)
Mill O' Forest Primary School, Stonehaven

Pollution

Litter everywhere
Smoke in the air
People stand and stare
But they don't care
Cars rushing by
Fumes in the sky
Some are chokin'
Lungs are broken
There's only one solution
We need a resolution
To cut down pollution
For the good of mankind.

Jamie Andrew (11)
Mill O' Forest Primary School, Stonehaven

Kelvin Hall

On the day I ran at Kelvin Hall,
I was so nervous but ended up having a ball.
The place was big and full of noise,
Full of people, most of them boys.

My race was called and the lanes were picked,
I was so scared I could have been sick.
We took our places and waited for the gun,
Then bang, it went, and we ran, ran, ran, ran.

I pushed and ran with all my might
I could see the race was going to be a fight,
I could see the finish getting nearer,
'Thank goodness,' I said, 'it's getting clearer.'

We cross the line, the race is done
And guess what I've *won, won, won.*

Stewart Clark (12)
Mill O' Forest Primary School, Stonehaven

Aeroplane

Big plane, magical and bright,
Red, green, blue and white.
Great big wings like a bird,
From a distance the engine is heard.

I walk in it and smell the curry,
The air hostess is in a hurry.
People getting their seat belts on
The pilot talking over the intercom.

Here we are near the end of the flight,
A man drooling, what a sight.
The pilot lets out the landing gear,
He lands it smoothly, we all cheer.

Stuart Saville (11)
Mill O' Forest Primary School, Stonehaven

First Netball Match

We leave our house,
We start to walk up,
We're so nervous,
We almost drop.

Then the bell rings,
Our first match is on,
Then in the end,
We finally won.

The crowd is watching,
We hear them cheer,
Not long after,
The final's here!

Running and shouting,
Booing we ignore,
Jumping and pivoting,
Then we score!

They said our team's name,
We all feared the worst,
Then we found out,
That we had come first!

Eilish Baird (12)
Mill O' Forest Primary School, Stonehaven

The Love Poem

Love is red like a red rose
Love sounds like birds singing in a tree
Love tastes like wedding cake
Love smells like new perfume
Love looks like a field of new flowers
Love feels like new petals on a flower
Love reminds me of my family.

Emma Gordon & Rhys Falconer (9)
Mill O' Forest Primary School, Stonehaven

Hurricane

It feels like a storm shaking like mad,
The ground falling apart,
My heart beating fast, ever so fast.

I hear rain, wind, thunder and lightning crashing off of stuff.
People screaming everywhere, running up and down the street.
People crying for parents to come.

I see people dead lying all over the place.
Coughing and screaming
Legs and arms broken,
Dead animals lying all over the place
     Cats
     Dogs
     Even
     Birds.

Deborah Ogilvie (10)
Mill O' Forest Primary School, Stonehaven

Party Time!

The lights are flashing
Everybody's moving
The music is lashing
We are all grooving.

There is party punch
And snacks all round
There's a lot too much
For only one pound.

It's coming to the end
Boy wasn't that fun?
We met up with friends
But now the party is done!

Kelly Muir (12)
Mill O' Forest Primary School, Stonehaven

Hate

Hate is black like darkness
Hate sounds like a black heart pumping black blood
Hate tastes like black soil
Hate smells like black foul breath
Hate looks like the crashing sea
Hate feels like black bruises on shivery skin
Hate reminds you of my nice brother
Who was lying in hospital with a black disease.

Billy Wilson (9)
Mill O' Forest Primary School, Stonehaven

Baseball

Lights, balls, players too,
Batters waiting for their cue,
Baseball diamonds, pitcher's mound,
Fans cheering their encouraging sound,
I step up, take my swing,
Crack! I hit the ball, the fans sing,
Over the fence the ball sails,
Home run! My team prevails.

Ethan Attwood (11)
Mill O' Forest Primary School, Stonehaven

Anger

Anger is amber like fire
Anger sounds like rumbling thunder
Anger tastes like fire in your mouth
Anger smells like burning wood
Anger looks like a red-hot devil
Anger feels like you've been stabbed by a fiery knife
Anger reminds me of a burning hot fire.

Kim Mellis (10)
Mill O' Forest Primary School, Stonehaven

Fear

Fear is black like the night sky
Fear sounds like witches screaming in your ears
Fear tastes like dryness and bitterness in your mouth
Fear smells like fire and burning
Fear looks like Darth Vader in a pure dark room with smoke
Fear feels like an empty room with smoke and steam
Fear reminds me of when my grandma Bunny died
And when my dad was in hospital.

Chloe Jackson (10)
Mill O' Forest Primary School, Stonehaven

Fear

Fear is black like the night sky
Fear sounds like a witch's scream
Fear tastes like sickness and numbness in my mouth
Fear smells like blood
Fear looks like a black room with dark staring eyes
Fear feels like a dark road that never stops going
Fear reminds me of the murder of my cousin's stepmum.

Kelly McLaren (10)
Mill O' Forest Primary School, Stonehaven

Love

Love is red like a rose
Love sounds like birds singing in a tree
Love tastes like strawberries and cream
Love smells like country air
Love looks like a field of flowers
Love feels like a petal of a flower
Love reminds me of my mum and dad.

Ryan Brown (9)
Mill O' Forest Primary School, Stonehaven

Hate

Hate is black like darkness,
Hate sounds like the wild seas of black death,
Hate tastes like black soil,
Hate smells like foul black breath,
Hate looks like black blood,
Hate feels like black bruises on shivery skin,
Hate reminds me of black scabs on someone's shin.

Rebecca McRobbie (10)
Mill O' Forest Primary School, Stonehaven

Anger

Anger is amber like fire,
Anger sounds like a rumble of thunder,
Anger tastes like fire in my mouth,
Anger smells like burning wood,
Anger looks like steam coming out of a kettle,
Anger feels like I'm going to explode,
Anger reminds me of my uncle Martin.

Sophie Christie (10)
Mill O' Forest Primary School, Stonehaven

Fear

Fear is black like the night sky
Fear sounds like a witch's scream
Fear tastes like dryness and sickness in your mouth
Fear smells like dust and smoke
Fear looks like red devils scaring little children
Fear feels like a dead empty room with devils in it
Fear reminds me of my friend helping me to be brave.

Tonicha Masson (9)
Mill O' Forest Primary School, Stonehaven

Fear

Fear is yellow if you are a coward
Fear sounds like your heart pumping blood through your veins
At a thousand miles an hour
Fear tastes like sick and clogs up your throat
It smells foul like the emotion that it is
Fear is quick and nippy
Fear feels cold and sends a shiver up your spine
Fear reminds me of yellow cowards
Which are scared of things like spiders.

John Campbell (10)
Mill O' Forest Primary School, Stonehaven

Hate

Hate is black like darkness.
Hate sounds like a black heart pumping black blood.
Hate tastes like black soil.
Hate smells like black foul breath.
Hate looks like the black wavy sea.
Hate feels like black bruises on shivery skin.
Hate reminds me of the black memory of me lying in a hospital bed
By myself, getting my tonsils out!

Kieran Paley (10)
Mill O' Forest Primary School, Stonehaven

Sadness

Sadness is blue like tears.
Sadness sounds like silence. Shh!
Sadness tastes like salted water.
Sadness smells like strong seaweed.
Sadness looks like a lonely river.
Sadness feels like I'm wet and cold.
Sadness reminds me of the true story, Titanic.

Connor Douglas (9) & Gemma Brown (11)
Mill O' Forest Primary School, Stonehaven

Happiness

Happiness, I feel, is a bright yellow.
The same colour as a Livestrong band
Or the sun on a light, hot and bright day.

Happiness feels like when my gran used to take my hand
When I was only four years old
And tell all the stories that she told.

Happiness tastes like fish and chips,
When you're sitting on a beach in Cornwall
Watching the waves rolling in and out,
With surfers out, not far offshore
Looking for places to go and explore.

Happiness smells like a newly baked cake
Sitting by a window on a china plate
Or the fresh bread made in Asda
Which smells like a sort of bakery!

Happiness looks like my gran's face,
When she's trying to fix my trainer's shoelace!
Or when my little brother, Bruce, is caught
To be it when he's playing duck, duck, goose!

Euan Dryburgh (10)
Mill O' Forest Primary School, Stonehaven

Hate

Hate is black like darkness.
Hate sounds like the black seas of death.
Hate tastes like black soil.
Hate smells like damp foul soil.
Hate looks like tears in the sea.
Hate feels like pain running down your back.
Hate reminds me of when my grandpa was lying in a hospital bed.

Katie Gordon (9)
Mill O' Forest Primary School, Stonehaven

Earthquake

Earthquake, I can see people running,
Running for their lives,
I can see buildings crashing to the floor,
I can see cracks everywhere leading to the down under.

Earthquake, I can feel rumbling like the rumble in my tummy,
I can feel crashing from falling buildings,
I can feel the screaming of the people.

Earthquake, I can hear the trains and cars
Coming off the roads and rails,
I can hear all the buildings tumbling to the floor
I can hear people screaming *'Earthquake!'*

Andrew Dart (10)
Mill O' Forest Primary School, Stonehaven

Drought

You can feel the hard rock on your feet,
You seem to hate every rock you meet.
It really hurts, it sometimes gives you scabs,
And it makes you very mad.

You can see nothing because it's empty, nothing's there
You can't see anything, it is bare!

You can't hear anything
It's completely empty, no water left
It's such a pest.
It's very tiring, no water to cool us down
And it makes us frown.

Cheri Brown (10)
Mill O' Forest Primary School, Stonehaven

Football Match

Large crowds walking down the road, all in their own little mode.
All the people wearing scarves and gloves, a large crowd shoves.
Everyone rushing through the toll, to see the score of a goal.

Players marching through the tunnel, in the background a ship's
funnel.
The roar of the crowd, you could just tell the manager was proud.
All the different coloured tops, that had been bought from very
large shops.
The ball spun through the air, but where it was going, they did not
care.

A fight broke out and everyone started to shout.
The referee started calling, but everyone was brawling.
A child was hit, his mother took a fit.
The police came and marched the men away in shame.

In the dressing room players cried, but when the police came in
They all lied.
Everyone was bruised and battered, some people's things broken
And tattered.
The players slowly sneaked back on the pitch,
But one of the players saw a person who looked like a witch.
The referee blew his whistle, some people were holding a Scottish
thistle.

The players re-took kick-off but one of the fans had a very loud cough.
One of the players took a shot, the keeper just stood still like a robot.
The match finished and everyone was cold, but still in one second
All their strips were sold.

Sam Gutteridge (11)
Mill O' Forest Primary School, Stonehaven

Anger

Anger is amber like fire
Anger sounds like rumbling thunder
Anger tastes like fireballs in your mouth
Anger smells like burning wood
Anger looks like a red-hot devil
Anger feels like you've been stabbed by a fiery sword
Anger reminds me of being accused of stuff that I didn't do.

Shannon Smith (9)
Mill O' Forest Primary School, Stonehaven

Fear

Fear is pure black like the night sky,
Fear sounds like a devil's roaring laugh,
Fear tastes like dryness in your mouth,
Fear smells like burning sparks,
Fear looks like the Devil slaying the angel,
Fear feels like you're going to explode and your soul
Will burst into tiny pieces.
Fear reminds me of when I nearly got run over by a car.

Kirsty Thomson (9)
Mill O' Forest Primary School, Stonehaven

Love

Love is red like roses.
Love sounds like birds singing in a tree.
Love tastes like strawberries and cream.
Love smells like new flowers in a field.
Love feels like a girl kissing my cheek.
Love reminds me of my old girlfriend's hairspray in England.

Kieran Johnson (9)
Mill O' Forest Primary School, Stonehaven

Anger

Anger is amber like fire.
Anger sounds like rumbling thunder.
Anger tastes like jalapeno in your mouth.
Anger smells like burning wood.
Anger looks like a red-hot flame.
Anger feels like someone stabbing you in the back.
Anger reminds me of my old cat!

Jonathan Penman (9)
Mill O' Forest Primary School, Stonehaven

Sadness

Sadness is blue like tears.
Sadness sounds like silence.
Sadness tastes like salty water.
Sadness smells like the sea.
Sadness looks like a lonely river.
Sadness feels like I'm wet and cold.
Sadness reminds me of the story of the Titanic sinking.

Rachael Craig (9)
Mill O' Forest Primary School, Stonehaven

Love

Love is red like a red rose
Love sounds like a heart beating
Love tastes like a wedding cake
Love smells like new perfume
Love looks like a field of flowers
Love feels like a new petal on a flower
Love reminds me of my dad's aftershave before he died.

Lee Ramage (10)
Mill O' Forest Primary School, Stonehaven

Tsunami

I can hear the waves crashing on the shore and killing people.
About 100 million or less, it's sad and annoying.

I can see people praying to survive and not get killed.
By the tsunami or the big wave, people are crying and screaming,
It's miserable.

I can feel my heart thumping and going faster and faster.
Am I going to die?
The sun is boiling me to death.

Denzel Bruce (10)
Mill O' Forest Primary School, Stonehaven

Sadness

Sadness is blue like tears
Sadness sounds like silence
Sadness tastes like salty water
Sadness smells like strong seaweed
Sadness looks like a lonely river
Sadness feels like I'm wet and cold
Sadness reminds me of the Titanic sinking.

Stuart Moir (9)
Mill O' Forest Primary School, Stonehaven

Fear

Fear is pure black like the night sky
Fear sounds like a witch's cackle
Fear tastes like sickness in your mouth
Fear smells like sparks from a burning fire
Fear looks like a devil drinking blood in pure darkness
Fear reminds me of the time I got lost at the beach.

Charlie Malcolm (10)
Mill O' Forest Primary School, Stonehaven

Love

Love is like a red rose
Love sounds like a bluebird in a tree
Love tastes like my sweet home
Love smells like a new flower
Love looks old fashioned
Love feels like a dove
Love reminds me of my family.

Tara Hector (9)
Mill O' Forest Primary School, Stonehaven

Fear

Fear is black like the night sky,
Fear sounds like a witch's cackle,
Fear tastes like dryness in your mouth,
Fear smells like warm blood,
Fear looks like a vampire sucking blood,
Fear feels like a devil sucking out your soul,
Fear reminds me of pure darkness.

Caitlin Imray (10)
Mill O' Forest Primary School, Stonehaven

Hate

Hate is black like darkness.
Hate sounds like the black seas of death.
Hate tastes like black soil.
Hate smells like damp foil.
Hate looks like tears in the sea.
Hate feels like you're getting lonely.
Hate reminds me of my granda dying.

Zoe Davidson (9)
Mill O' Forest Primary School, Stonehaven

Anger Poem

Anger is amber like a blazing fire.
Anger sounds like rumbling thunder.
Anger tastes like hot fireballs in your mouth.
Anger smells like stinging, burning wood.
Anger looks like a sizzling, red-hot devil.
Anger feels like someone has just stabbed you in the back.
Anger reminds me of rippling red wine that my nana used to drink.

Lauren Gerrard (11)
Mill O' Forest Primary School, Stonehaven

Fear

Fear is black like the night sky.
Fear sounds like screaming in your ear.
Fear tastes like a bitter feeling.
Fear smells like mouldy cheese peeling.
Fear looks like a shocking face.
Fear feels like you're losing your pace.
Fear reminds me of a scary movie I have seen.

Christopher Hunt (11)
Mill O' Forest Primary School, Stonehaven

Sadness

Sadness is blue like tears
Sadness sounds like silence
Sadness tastes like salty water
Sadness smells like strong seaweed
Sadness looks like a lonely river
Sadness feels like I'm wet and cold
Sadness reminds me of the day I cried

Rachel Eastcroft (10)
Mill O' Forest Primary School, Stonehaven

Love

Love is red like a red rose
Love sounds like birds singing in a tree
Love tastes like treacle pudding
Love smells like fresh country air
Love looks like a field of new flowers
Love feels like new petals growing on a flower
Love reminds me of lots of people being together.

Jenni Ogg (10)
Mill O' Forest Primary School, Stonehaven

Hate

Hate is black like darkness
Hate sounds like the black seas of death
Hate tastes like black soil
Hate smells like damp foul soil
Hate looks like tears in the sea
Hate feels like you want to be sick
Hate reminds me of my grandad's funeral.

Chloe Christie (10)
Mill O' Forest Primary School, Stonehaven

Sadness

Sadness is blue like tears
Sadness sounds like silence
Sadness tastes like salty water
Sadness smells like strong seaweed
Sadness looks like a lonely river
Sadness feels like I'm wet and cold
Sadness reminds me of the Titanic.

Craig Forbes (10)
Mill O' Forest Primary School, Stonehaven

In The Flood!

What can you hear?
I can hear the water rushing round the streets.
I can hear the water splashing round my feet.
Can you hear it too?

What can you feel?
I can feel the water soaking all my feet.
I can feel the water rising up my feet.
Can you feel it too?

What can you see?
I can see the water rushing everywhere.
I can't see the emergency services anywhere!
Can you see it too?

Can you see the emergency services?
Was it a hoax?
Probably those silly folks!
Is that what delayed them?

Francesca Ballard (11)
Mill O' Forest Primary School, Stonehaven

Flooding

The water rises as the rain falls
I can see the water getting tall
I can hear the pit pat of the rain
Rushing down a hill blocking a drain.

When I'm in the water I can feel
The wetness beneath my hands
And I feel everything apart from the land,
Now the rain is over I can breathe
That's it, gone into the sea.

Greig Clark (11)
Mill O' Forest Primary School, Stonehaven

Flooding

I can see people running for shelter and benches and tables are wet.
Clothes are dripping wet, cold and miserable,
Rain is getting heavy and hard.
People are shouting and rivers are getting higher.

You can hear people shouting and unhappy.
The rain very heavy and hard.
Windows closing
The sea crashes down
Cars then leave the town.
Curtains closing.

You feel wet, cold and scared of people running.
I cannot wait to get home
My dog has run away and no one else is there.
I am on the pathway home through the forest.

Michelle Ingram (11)
Mill O' Forest Primary School, Stonehaven

Flooding!

Here it comes, a great flood, water splashing, water killing,
Men and women screaming.
Children hurling, houses crumbling, bricks splashing.

I can feel burning in my body,
Sadness and selfishness.
I'm watching from my room as people cry and drown.
I wish I could save all those poor and scared children.

I can see helicopters, boats and planes,
Animals moving, sheep are drowning, thugs are frowning.
Elders fleeing and youngsters pleading for their adults saving and
water throwing.

Murray Cheyne (10)
Mill O' Forest Primary School, Stonehaven

A Love Poem

Love is like a pink, lush rose
Planted in a country field,
It feels like a silk cloth
But something you can't wield.

Love tastes like beautiful chocolate
That someone has taken time with,
Love smells like a whiff of perfume
In a bottle that you can give.

Love looks like thin air
Something you cannot see
Love sounds like the harmony of music
That is played by you and me.

James Johnson (10)
Mill O' Forest Primary School, Stonehaven

Rainforest

In the rainforest you can feel
Little leaves tickling your heels,
Then you think it is a snake,
You begin to shake.

In the rainforest you can see
Little monkeys in the tree,
Then you see a little birdie
Running from a bee, *bzz! Bzz!*

In the rainforest you can hear
Heaps and heaps of fear
Argh! Argh! You scream
You think they are your friend.

Scott Webster (10)
Mill O' Forest Primary School, Stonehaven

Tsunami

Hear
In a tsunami you can
Hear the waves splashing, crashing.
In a tsunami you can hear people shouting,
Screaming for help and houses crashing down.

Feel
You know you're scared, terrified,
Your heart pumps faster and faster
You feel like a flower sprouted,
All alone in a street with no one there.

See
When a tsunami comes
You can see houses crash in a flash.
People screaming for their life!
A tsunami is like a scary, raging monster.

Gemma Gerrard (11)
Mill O' Forest Primary School, Stonehaven

Earthquake

I can see the Earth cracking
I can see the waves crashing
I can see people running
I can see what is coming!

I can feel the Earth rumbling
I can feel the Earth crumbling
I can feel the buildings tumbling
I can feel the cars smashing.

I can hear people screaming
I can hear the cars crashing
I can hear buildings crumbling
I think it must be an
Earthquake!

Robyn Munro (11)
Mill O' Forest Primary School, Stonehaven

Drought

I can see the ground breaking up because all the water has gone.
As it breaks up houses and homes start to shake.

I can hear the screaming and shouting of people and barking of dogs.
Crashing, banging and clattering of houses and sheds falling to the
ground.
The clattering of greenhouses and windows smashing.

I can feel shaking cracks in the ground
And the heavy beat of my heart because I'm so scared.

Zoe Taylor (10)
Mill O' Forest Primary School, Stonehaven

Anger

Most people are angry at each other.
Anger is red or purple and really very dark
You feel stressed and feel like you want to hit someone.
It reminds me of when you're down and sad.
It sounds like volcanoes and fireworks.
It tastes like dry gums and it's hard to swallow.
It smells of smoke and sweat and food.
You look like a red mushroom, really red and hot.
People stare at you and laugh.

Becky Bruce (11)
Mill O' Forest Primary School, Stonehaven

Love

Love is pink and red like roses freshly picked
It smells like perfume that sweetens the air.
It reminds me of cosy, soft, romantic things.
It sounds like crying laughter and little love songs.
It looks like hugs and kisses.
It feels like paradise and fun for almost everyone.
Love is amazing, the best (or worst) thing in life.

Ashleigh Hunter (11)
Mill O' Forest Primary School, Stonehaven

Hurricane

In a hurricane you feel a big, big vibration.
Crumples your heartbeat like a storm and a bump in the ground.
A big balloon goes up in the air,
And a bang in your heart, scared and unhappy.

I see everyone fly in the air and back down again and my hands
Toss and turn about.
I flip and kick but can't get away.
I see people die on this Earth because of this very bad hurricane.

You hear bang, bang from people,
And boom-boom, boom-boom from your heart,
And from everyone comes a scream.
Everyone hears the screams.

David Craigmyle (10)
Mill O' Forest Primary School, Stonehaven

Friendship

It tastes like a juicy pear, tasty and sweet
It looks like my mum, she's special and beautiful
It smells like a home-made apple pie, sweet, warm and delicious.
It feels like freshly cut grass, lovely and soft.
It reminds me of my mum taking me to the bike park
Because it makes me happy.

Alan Rae (8)
Nethermains Primary School, Denny

Friendship

Friendship is gold like sand from the beach.
It tastes like tasty mango.
It looks like people running.
It smells like cherry pie that's just come out of the oven.
It feels as soft as a kitten.
It reminds me of the first time I made friends.

Daniel Guy (9)
Nethermains Primary School, Denny

Friendship

Friendship is like a rainbow, each colour represents a
Best friend or a friend.

It tastes like a pot of cherries and strawberries with
Strawberry syrup.

Friendship looks like a beautiful beach
It smells like honey.

It feels like soft teddy bears.

It reminds me of funny memories like the one when
Kieran fell off my swing and lots more.

Mairi Soldatic (8)
Nethermains Primary School, Denny

Friendship

Friendship is red like a ring of fire that can never break us up.
It tastes like a juicy red apple.
It looks like a little newborn bunny.
It smells like honey from a beehive.
It feels soft like a fluffy little dog.
It reminds me of when I first saw my mum.

Christopher Mullan (8)
Nethermains Primary School, Denny

Friendship

Friendship is red like a rose.
It tastes like hot apple pie when it comes out of the oven.
It looks like everyone has a smile on their face.
It smells like a garden of beautiful flowers.
It feels soft and fluffy like a teddy bear.
It reminds me of my mum.

Caitlyn Ross (8)
Nethermains Primary School, Denny

Friendship

Friendship is yellow like in the summer when you play
With your friends in the roasting hot sun.

It sounds like laughter, you and your friends having lots
Of fun.

It tastes like a pear.

It looks like happiness, you and your friends having lots of fun.

It smells like sweet, sugary, chocolate strawberries.

It feels like rain dropping on you and your friend.

It reminds me of my pet Fluffy.

Nicole Wilson (9)
Nethermains Primary School, Denny

Friendship

Friendship is gold like playing on the sand on the beach.
It tastes sweet like the pink candyfloss we eat together.
It looks like the sun shining down on us playing.
It sounds like music when we're dancing.
It smells like bright red roses in the garden.
It feels like teddy bears lovely and soft.
It reminds me of my old friends on holiday.

Emma Wilson (9)
Nethermains Primary School, Denny

Friendship

Friendship is yellow like playing in the sun with my friend.
It tastes sweet like strawberries.
It looks like people playing together having fun.
It smells like hot apple pie just out of the oven.
It feels like the rain falling from the sky.
It reminds me of my dog Skye.

Amy Weir (8)
Nethermains Primary School, Denny

Friendship

Friendship is green like grass we can play football on.
It tastes sweet like banana milkshake.
It looks like playing tig in the house.
It smells like chocolate when you open it.
It tastes delicious like cheese pizza.
It feels like I'm happy as could be.
It sounds like laughing all the time.
It reminds me of playing with my dad.

Jordan Mitchell (8)
Nethermains Primary School, Denny

Friendship

Friendship is baby blue like waves coming in from the ocean.
It tastes like a big, juicy strawberry.
It smells like flowers growing in the field.
It looks like rain dripping from the trees.
It sounds like children giggling together.
It feels soft and cuddly like a big bear.
It reminds me of bouncing on my first trampoline
When I was small.

Charley Shanks (9)
Nethermains Primary School, Denny

Friendship

Friendship is orange like the beautiful leaves that you see in autumn.
It tastes like a pineapple swirl with sugar on top.
It looks like a funky garden me and my girlfriends play in.
It smells like toffee covered in boiled chocolate sauce.
It feels like being at the beach with a barbecue and sand blowing
                                             everywhere.
It reminds me of the first time I met my best friend.

Hannah Shade (8)
Nethermains Primary School, Denny

Dreams

I've always wanted to go to space and
To complete the human race.

All my friends think this too,
So believe me it's totally true.

To see the red planet it's called Mars
And to travel around the silver stars.

To go in a rocket it's my dream and to meet
The NASA space team.

Sitting in front of the bright silver moon
That shines like the handle of a new silver spoon.

Please, oh please make this true
I want it and you might too.

Lauren Baillie (11)
Nethermains Primary School, Denny

Anger

Anger sounds like an explosive volcano erupting.
Anger feels like a mane of a lion.
Anger tastes like boiling lava from a volcano.
Anger smells like French cheese in the fridge.
Anger looks like birds eating their prey.
Anger reminds me of people drowning in the sea.

Robert Macalister (10)
Nethermains Primary School, Denny

Laughter

Laughter sounds like children playing in a park.
Laughter feels like a blue silk dress.
Laughter tastes like a coconut cake.
Laughter smells like cream roses in a flower shop.
Laughter reminds me of my pink fluffy pillow.

Terri Valentine (11)
Nethermains Primary School, Denny

Fun!

Fun sounds like children on the rides.
Fun feels like ladybirds crawling up your arm.
Fun smells like delicious melted chocolate on toast.
Fun looks like opening presents at Christmas time.
Fun tastes like hard and crunchy mints.
Fun reminds me of my mum and dad's 40th birthday party.

Caroline Docherty (10)
Nethermains Primary School, Denny

Happiness

Happiness sounds like my mum and dad laughing.
Happiness feels like an excellent birthday present.
Happiness smells like my mum's absolutely amazing cooking.
Happiness looks like all of my fabulous family.
Happiness tastes like my mum's perfect cooking.
Happiness reminds me of my first day at school.

Cameron Sweeney (10)
Nethermains Primary School, Denny

Anger

Anger sounds like a tiger roaring at its prey
Anger feels like people stamping over you
Anger smells like a jar of out of date pickles
Anger looks like a fight between two lions
Anger tastes like vinegar in your mouth
Anger reminds me of a nasty fight.

David Gemmell (10)
Nethermains Primary School, Denny

Sadness

Sadness sounds like teardrops falling.
Sadness feels like wet damp clothes in from the rain.
Sadness smells like smelly bins in the bin shed.
Sadness looks like people waving goodbye.
Sadness tastes like horrible mushy peas.
Sadness reminds me of being unwell.

Linzi Davidson (11)
Nethermains Primary School, Denny

Laughter

Laughter sounds like lovely little birds chirping.
Laughter feels like a furry rug on my floor.
Laughter looks like children playing in the playground.
Laughter tastes like strawberry chewing gum.
Laughter reminds me of all my school friends and my teacher.

Jodie Kane (11)
Nethermains Primary School, Denny

Laughter

Laughter sounds like children playing in the sun.
Laughter feels like bubbly chocolate.
Laughter smells like roses in my garden.
Laughter looks like the sunshine on a sunny day.
Laughter tastes like sweet strawberries.
Laughter reminds me of funny jokes.

Danielle McAteer (10)
Nethermains Primary School, Denny

Honour

Honour sounds like a brave soldier at war.
Honour feels like the middle of a battlefield.
Honour smells like a fresh foggy morning.
Honour looks like a boy standing up to a bully.
Honour tastes like winning the war.
Honour reminds me of my grandad Eddie.

Daryl MacMillan (10)
Nethermains Primary School, Denny

Anger

Anger looks like a destructive tornado.
Anger feels like prickly hedgehogs.
Anger sounds like people screaming.
Anger smells like manure in the fields.
Anger tastes like dirt when you fall.
Anger reminds me of unhappy memories.

Craig Fulton (10)
Nethermains Primary School, Denny

Happiness

Happiness sounds like the New Year's Eve bell ringing.
Happiness smells like melting milk chocolate.
Happiness tastes like French cheese.
Happiness looks like children playing in the park.
Happiness reminds me of fun times at the fair.

Gary Collier (10)
Nethermains Primary School, Denny

Anger

Anger sounds like the enraged wrath of fork lightning.
Anger feels like the scorching feel of a hot cooker.
Anger smells like the hideous smell of melted cheese.
Anger looks like the horrifying look of a heated fire.
Anger tastes like the nasty taste of tomatoes.
Anger reminds me of a raging, erupting volcano.

Alexander Fullard (10)
Nethermains Primary School, Denny

Holiday

I flew in the plane
To sunny Spain
The weather's good
So is the food
It was all good
Till my brother went in a mood
I didn't have fun
Or play in the sun
Our parents sent us to our room
Forget a holiday
It's all doom and gloom!

Daniel McPhillips (11)
Nethermains Primary School, Denny

Anger

Anger sounds like a bubbling, erupting volcano.
Anger smells like used gunfire.
Anger tastes like horrible disgusting blood.
Anger looks like the waves crashing in.
Anger reminds me of *anger!*

Jacqueline Huskie (11)
Nethermains Primary School, Denny

My Idol

My idol is Nacho Novo,
He plays for Ranger's Football Club.
25 goals,
And never hits the poles.
With his black spiky hair,
He always plays fair.
He doesn't mind being small,
As long as he can kick a ball.
Nacho is from Spain,
Where it will never rain.
Novo loves playing for Rangers,
And all the fans cheer him on.
Novo has special boots,
That help him score lots of goals.
I'm the biggest fan of Nacho Novo,
And he is the number pro.
I hope he stays at Rangers
For ever and ever!

Jodie Butler (12)
Nethermains Primary School, Denny

Hope And Despair

Hope
Hope is a bright star shining in the black sky.
It is the love in my heart.
It is the cure to all illnesses.
It is as sweet as a tender ice cream.

Despair
Despair is as black as the night sky with no light.
It tastes like raw chicken.
It smells like smoke.
It lives in all evil.
It is the heart of all evil.

Argyle Ryan (12)
Nethermains Primary School, Denny

The Team

The team trained hard
Emotions boiled over,
Fights broke out.
The game was drawing closer
And everyone was nervous,
The coach announced the team
For many it was the end of a cup final dream.
Some players jumped with happiness,
Others cried with sadness.
The day of the game had come,
In the dressing room we saw,
The fear on the players' faces,
And the sweat running off their heads.
The ref's whistle blew,
The players knew it was time to go,
Shaking and scared they walked down the narrow tunnel.
Ninety minutes is near approaching,
We were winning 2-0
The final whistle blew,
The team and the crowd went crazy,
We had done it,
We were the champions!

Ross McNeil (12)
Nethermains Primary School, Denny

Friendship

Friendship is light blue like the sky,
It tastes like strawberry ice cream.
It looks like the sun.
It smells like Lynx spray
It feels like playing in the wind
It reminds me of my friend Jaime.

Jayjay Allen (9)
Nethermains Primary School, Denny

In School

S is for success
C is for children you need for a school
O is for organisation for school
O is for over-working in school
L is for lunch, hooray, we're away from the teacher.
T is for teachers ever so boring
E is for education
A is for algebra
C is for chemistry
E is for early learning
R is for religion we learn in RME
P is for pupils ever so smart
U is for understanding lessons
P is for preparation
I is for intelligence
L is for learning new things.

Stacie Hunter (12)
Nethermains Primary School, Denny

Opposite Sides

Anger is scarlet-red,
It smells like burning rubber.
It tastes like red chillies,
And feels like a sharp bit of metal.
Anger sounds like a lightning storm,
It lives in everyone.

Calm is pure white,
It smells like a rose.
It tastes like a bar of chocolate,
And feels like a bit of silk.
Calm sounds like the sea,
It lives at the seaside.

Liam Wright (11)
Nethermains Primary School, Denny

A Magical Place

I was sitting in my room
CD player going boom-boom
My door opened, I got a fright
I did not know what was in my sight
I was as scared as can be
It was only my mum calling for me.

Jumping and swerving down the stairs
Hoping I'm not in a dragon's lair
When all of a sudden I got a fright
I thought I was having a heart attack,
I landed in a darkened room
No CDs going boom-boom,
I knew it wasn't just my mum
Then I heard the beat of the drum.

The people said, 'We come in peace'
The leader was called Liam Reece
He said, 'I only want to be your friend
I'll be with you 'til the end.
If you don't want to play with me,
I'll send you home as safe as can be.'

So there I was back in my room
CD player going boom-boom
I know now I'm here to stay
I'm far too tired to go to play
So night-night,
Sleep tight
Don't let the bedbugs bite.

Siobhan Clark (11)
Nethermains Primary School, Denny

High School

Turning the corners in life I know
High school is coming
Here I go
There will be good times
And bad, happy
And sad
Some things I just can't change.

It's no longer in the distance
It's getting closer and closer
Just a few months to go.

I can't help feeling scared
I know I just have to go.

Emma Marshall (11)
Nethermains Primary School, Denny

Two Sides

Hope is a heavenly white.
It smells like gorgeous perfume
And tastes like chocolate strawberries.
Hope sounds like you have won something
And it lives in your heart.

Despair is a black bat
It smells like burning smoke
And tastes like raw chicken.
Despair sounds like nails running down the blackboard
It feels like getting hurt by a friend
And lives in a dark corner.

Taylor Brown (12)
Nethermains Primary School, Denny

The Fairground

Roller coaster
Merry-go-round
Log flume
In the fairground.

Food court
Go-Karts
Water parks
In the fairground.

Big stalls
Big prizes
Lots of people
In the fairground.

Late nights
Bright lights
Great fun
At the fairground.

Early morning
No people around
All chained up
No more fairground.

Colin Mackay (12)
Nethermains Primary School, Denny

Scotland

S is for the brave Scots
C is for the country we live in
O is for all the old castles
T is for the tartan army
L is for the lovely land it is
A is for all the battles Scotland won
N is for the monster Nessie
D is for Dundee.

Scot Cameron (11)
Nethermains Primary School, Denny

Eco-Day

I see a bunch of children all in rows,
I see clouds as white as snow.
I can see roses as red as fire,
The sky as blue as bluebells.

I feel really excited,
I feel warm,
I feel the sand in my hand,
I can feel the sticky glue.
I feel as happy as Larry.

I can hear children screaming,
I can hear rustling of the trees.
I can hear the wind whistle past my ears,
I hear the music of the keep-fit,
I can hear the adults muttering to each other.

Rhys Park (11)
Newarthill Primary School, Newarthill

Eco-Day

I see flowers and green grass
I see the sky blue and pink
I see children running around mad
While teachers do workshops
Like art, gardening and keep-fit.

I feel overjoyed, excited and happy
I feel calm but mad,
I feel sticky as the glue melts and dries
Onto my hands and the sand on the top
Water and soap to take it away.

I hear voices over voices
And teachers saying 'Quiet!'
My head is aching
So Eco-Day was a good day and a great
Day to play.

Sarah Smith (11)
Newarthill Primary School, Newarthill

Eco-Day

I can see children bustling about,
Adults trying to keep order,
As the crowds increase more and more,
I look out the window and trees sway in
The wind,
I see the blue sky sway in the wind.

I feel cold as the wind sweeps about my ankles,
My heart is beating with excitement,
Amazed as we get photographed
And put in the papers.

I hear silence as the children work,
With occasional questions,
The wind whistles outside,
Children yell as they are late for
Workshops.

Abigail Grover (11)
Newarthill Primary School, Newarthill

Eco-Day

On Eco-Day there were lots of people wandering about,
Just wondering where to go,
What to see and what to do,
Everybody could see a blue and green thing waving abut,
It was the Eco-Flag.

I could feel the creepy-crawlies,
That were crawling all around,
Then I could feel the golden sand,
That was falling on my hand,
It was for the fossils we were making.

I could hear the children crying,
But they were not sad,
It was tears of laughter,
I could hear the rustling of trees,
When I was in the garden.

Kirstin Donnelly (11)
Newarthill Primary School, Newarthill

Eco-Day

I see children planting pansies as purple as royalty.
I see leaves as green as envy
And as new as the first grape of the season.
I look up into the sky, there is no sun
Just a dark swarm of clouds
As grey as a grandpa's hair but still as fluffy as a lamb.

I look down, the ground is littered with bark.
I can feel the moist soft soil but very damp.
I pull my hand onto the bench the wood is as hard as brick.
I rush over to the plastic plant pot
It's sharp and pointy.

The birds fly in and out trees twittering very sweetly,
But it gets louder almost to a screech and it's annoying.
The children who have voices like foghorns are shouting.
The leaves are rustling along the floor.

Emma King (11)
Newarthill Primary School, Newarthill

A Day Away

It was one bright sunny morning when it was our Eco-Day.
I could see buds as beautiful as a painting
And a bunch of children all in rows.
I could see our red and black school
With all the children co-ordinated.

The only thing I can say about how I felt is happy,
Happy as Larry.
Me and my friends all touching plants
As green as grass.
I could feel the roughness of P3's sand along my hand.

I could hear lots of children screaming
And the sound of the bell ringing in our ears.
I could hear the teacher shouting to see if we were
Ready to come into class.

Allyson Stevely (11)
Newarthill Primary School, Newarthill

Eco-Day

I see beautiful flowers of many colours,
Lots of children with their mothers
I see lots of children having fun
And the beautiful scorching sun,
I see lots of trees with green leaves
And a few yellow bees.

I feel the cool, cool air
And it feels like a teddy bear
I am craving with excitement
And joyous delight
I feel loads of happiness
And when it's halfway I feel restless.

I hear the rustle of the leaves
On all the very tall trees
I hear the birds singing away
And all the trees doing a sway
But best of all
I hear the *echo-call!*

Brian Flynn (11)
Newarthill Primary School, Newarthill

Eco-Day

I see some men putting us into rows
I see some plants as green as grass and being surrounded by trees
The sun beaming on them
It was a lovely day for planting
We were all waiting with our gloves and boots on.

We were all happy and we couldn't wait to get planting
We then got put into groups and told what to do
Then we got planting
When we saw dead maggots we gave them to Mrs Smith
She was bug hunting.

We can hear the whistling of the wind and the children having fun.

Tiffany Matthews (11)
Newarthill Primary School, Newarthill

Eco-Day

I can see the children running back and forth
I can feel the smooth sand slipping through my fingers
I can hear the radio buzzing away as we paint.

I can see the children creeping about slyly in the garden
I can feel my feet sinking into the mud of the garden
I can hear the men sweeping the path which the mucky children
Trail their feet along.

I can see the visitors walking to their cars
I feel dull that it is all over
I could hear nothing but silence

All was still and quiet
I could no longer hear or see anyone
No longer could I enjoy the laughing and giggling of Eco-Day.

Laura Hill (11)
Newarthill Primary School, Newarthill

Eco-Day

I could see people, visitors
Going round the workshops.

Children were playing in the mud
With snails, worms, slugs and all
And the plants as pink as pink could be.

I felt excited, weird but happy
Eyes looking at us at all times
I could feel the presence of people I didn't even know,
And I could feel the excitement all round.

I could hear adults talking, children too
A guide dog barking, what can I do?
I could hear the rustling of soil,
The clattering of forks and spades.
We planted the flowers which brings happiness too.

Nicola Blair (11)
Newarthill Primary School, Newarthill

Eco-Day

Blossom on the trees,
Blossom on the ground,
Plants with bumblebees,
And plants all around.
I see children planting,
With the soothing sound of birds chanting.

I feel a daffodil,
I feel the sun,
My feelings inside are still and fun.
I feel warm,
I feel cosy,
At least today was not so snowy.

My heart is beating, it's not hard to hear,
I hear the children's screaming laughter,
I hear the visitors' happy cheer,
I know there's fun now and after.
Eco-Days here every year.

Adee Cook (12)
Newarthill Primary School, Newarthill

A Good Day

I can see a big, bright, warm sun,
Yellow, orange, purple carnations,
I can also see bright yellow daffodils,
And pink buds starting to bloom on the trees,
I can see lots of different visitors walking about.

I can feel the cold, gritty soil out in the garden,
I can also feel the rough sand in my hand,
There is a cool breeze in the air but a nice breeze,
Everyone feels as happy as Larry.

I can hear the loud beating music from keep-fit,
I can also hear the birds tweeting and singing out in the garden,
The trees are rustling,
And all of the little children are very noisy with excitement.

Colleen Hughes (11)
Newarthill Primary School, Newarthill

Eco-Day

I see . . .
Children running round the hall,
Visitors coming in the main door.
Pupils refilling the garden plant pots.
Children being herded like sheep,
The infants cooking lovely treats.

I feel . . .
The gritty sand in the art class,
And the sticky glue we put on last.
The soft petals on the buttonhole flowers.
Warm and stuffy and tired in class,
Bored out my skull, I hope time flies past.

I hear . . .
Children talking as they wait in line,
Trees rustling as they clean up outside.
Visitors having conversations with each other.
Keep-fit music blaring in the hall,
Pupils with garden tools banging on the wall.

Fiona Wellcoat (11)
Newarthill Primary School, Newarthill

Eco-Day

I see . . .
I see men digging in the garden
And pupils in the classes.
I see the brightness of the sun,
Glaring down on the grass,
And the trees rustling in the wind.

I feel . . .
I feel the wind blowing onto my clothes,
And through my hair and on my face.
I feel happy because there is no work
Like language, maths and writing,
And I feel glad because I'm not sad.

I hear . . .
I hear music from keep-fit
And from recycled instruments.
I hear the wind whistling in the air,
With all the different leaves,
And the bell to move on to a different activity.

Jason Hattie (11)
Newarthill Primary School, Newarthill

Eco-Day

I see children, adults, visitors too,
I see a guide dog, lots of little bugs.
I see the plants that people brought,
I see pink and white blossoms blowing against my face.
I see this all on Eco-Day.

I feel wet, moist soil,
I feel white, stringy roots.
I feel lovely, soft, velvet-like hairs of an Alsatian
As I gently stroke its back and stomach,
I feel the wind blowing blossoms
Into my long black, loose hair
While blowing it out of place.
I feel this all on Eco-Day.

I hear trees and blossoms rustling
Autumn leaves crunching as I walk into the school garden
I hear children shouting like foghorns.
I hear loud beating music from keep-fit in the hall,
I hear Stephanie screaming as a big hairy spider crawls up her leg.
I hear this all on Eco-Day.

Aryana Motaghian (11)
Newarthill Primary School, Newarthill

Springtime

S pring-cleaning in your house
P olishing the TV and the table
R acing rabbits running in the grassy field
 I nsects crawling about on the trees
N ests with new birds and new lives
G reedily feeding from their mother
T rees with new buds live again
 I t's what we learn about, that's what it is
M uch more sun and that's what we like
E ach new day brings fun and joy.

Grant Rollo (10)
New Elgin Primary School, New Elgin

Springtime

S pringtime is fun when it is sunny and bright
P etals growing bright and beautiful. Petals green and
  Rain falling on top
R abbits and bunnies running round the tree looking at
  The beautiful flowers
I n springtime, fox cubs play and make people laugh.
  Some cubs run through the flowers.
N ests on trees with birds in them, looking up at the nice
  Colours in the sky
G reen grass in the fields, seeing chicks running and jumping
  Round the field. That makes you feel nice
T ulips with beautiful colours that make you smile and laugh
I t was spring when I saw lambs in their field running round
  The nice green grass
M ooing calves living in the nice green grass
E aster comes in the nice weather and that is when the piglets
  Are born.

Robert Forsyth (9)
New Elgin Primary School, New Elgin

Springtime

S inging birds in the beautiful green trees
P retty daffodils growing up
R inging bells while churches open
I n and out of woods picking bluebells
N ever ever going inside
G reat daisy chains being made
T ulips swaying in the breeze
I nto a puff the wind passes by
M akes the pansies grow so high
E verything sparkles in this great season.
  It's just too bad it comes once a year.

Ellice McCart (9)
New Elgin Primary School, New Elgin

Springtime

S pring is here, come out and see
P lay with me in the lovely sun
R abbits and bunnies are hopping all around the fields
I 'd like you to come and see the flowers
    The daisies, tulips, daffodils and even bluebells
    Multicoloured ones
N ew leaves have grown on the trees
G ood days have come now it is spring
T ime for very long evenings
I feel the wind go by
M ore people smile at this time of year
E aster is a very special day of the year.

Danielle Newlands (10)
New Elgin Primary School, New Elgin

Springtime

S pringtime is back, let's all do a dance,
P ansies and primroses grow up to the sky
R abbits sprint around the garden
I n and out the rabbits go through their burrows
N ew baby owlets being born, lots of other animals too
G rowing every day, they stay alive because of their mothers
T iny animals are following their mothers all over the place
I n the fields the flowers are more beautiful than ever
M oss is being used to make birds' nests
E veryone enjoys spring, especially me.

Abbie McKillop (9)
New Elgin Primary School, New Elgin

Springtime

S pringtime! Springtime! It's springtime again
P etals that are on the glamorous crocuses make you
　 Feel wonderful
R abbits that are following their mums and dads through
　 The khaki forest
I n the farmyard with all the friendly animals, playing in their straw
N ever miss a second of the sunshine
G ive the beautiful flowers some water to help them grow
T ime for cleaning your houses top to bottom
I t's time to fit in as much fun as you can.
　 Springtime is almost over
M any days have been filled with fun
E nd of spring and onto summer days.

Jack Byiers (9)
New Elgin Primary School, New Elgin

Springtime

S pringtime - sun all day long
P iglets drinking from their mother
R acing rabbits in the wood
I vy growing in gardens
N ew leaves growing on trees
G reen grass growing in gardens
T ime for chickens to lay eggs
I t's time to do spring-cleaning in your home
M agnificent fox cubs are born
E very day plants are planted.

Arran Johnston (10)
New Elgin Primary School, New Elgin

Springtime

S pringtime once again, the cold winter is now over
P laying longer in the evenings with all of your friends
R acing bunnies, rabbits in the field - a lovely sight
I n and out of their burrows in the warm sun
N ew growth on the trees, cool colours
G reen leaves and new buds all in different colours
T ulips are such nice colours - they are like the rainbows
   In the sky
I n the nests, fledging birds are going on their first flight
M ight be a little bumpy but it doesn't matter
E very newborn foal, fox cub and piglet are lovely and
   Everybody knows that springtime is a beautiful time of the year.

Blair Johnston (10)
New Elgin Primary School, New Elgin

Springtime

S unny days we like to go out and play
P iglets are running through fields of flowers like
   Primroses and pansies
R acing rabbits running with all the bunnies
I n spring we see lambs and calves
N ew leaves and blossom growing on trees
G reen grass growing for goats to eat
T he petals shining in the sun
I n my garden, I see flowers like daisies and daffodils
M ulticoloured packets of flowers
E aster egg hunts for the children.

Sophie Fraser (9)
New Elgin Primary School, New Elgin

Springtime

S pringtime sun shining down on a brand new world
P iglets are born and fed by their mothers
R unning through flowers like daffies and daisies
I dyllic views of flowers growing amongst the trees
N arcissus flowers grow just now, so do pansies,
   Poppies and primroses
G reen grass is growing quickly in gardens and the
   Flowers are beginning to bloom
T ea and cakes in the garden sitting on a blanket
I n all fields, baby animals are born and walk by their
   Mothers everywhere they go
M ooing calves living in the bright grassy fields
E very time it's springtime, you will love it night and day.

Billie Slinn (10)
New Elgin Primary School, New Elgin

Springtime

S un comes out during spring
P iglets are running about everywhere in the fields
R abbits are enjoying running about in the woods
I n springtime, people are enjoying the beach
N ew leaves are growing on the trees
G reen grass growing in the springtime
T iny insects and animals are growing
I n the spring, animals are running about everywhere
M um is doing the spring-cleaning
E aster is a day when people enjoy themselves.

John Stuart (10)
New Elgin Primary School, New Elgin

Springtime

S un is shining brightly in the pale blue sky
P retty petals growing in the sunny fields
R acing rabbits running quickly in the tall grassy fields
 I n spring, there are new lives all over the place
N esting birds singing in the huge trees
G reen grass sparkling in the sunny garden
T rees growing blossom in the blazing sun
 I vy sprouting brand new buds
M oss growing slowly on old houses with slated roofs
E aster chocolate eggs - tasty for your tum.

Shawn Sinclair (9)
New Elgin Primary School, New Elgin

Springtime

S pringtime - the sun reflecting off a
P ond. When the flowers bloom and the perfect
R ed sunset fills the sky with beautiful colours.
 I n the springtime you see the new trees blooming.
N ew life has begun in the world.
G oslings swimming happily in the pond.
T he petals on the flowers look so perfect.
 I n the garden there's colourful flowers that bloom.
M aybe all the things in springtime are perfect,
E aster is an important day of the year.

Michael Armstrong (10)
New Elgin Primary School, New Elgin

Springtime

S pringtime is a lovely time of year
P iglets and other animals are being born
R acing rabbits are running about
I n the gardens, insects are crawling all over the place
N ew animals feeding hungrily from their mother
G oslings swimming in the ponds
T ime for chickens to lay their eggs
I n spring lambs play in the fields
M agnificent fox cubs are being born
E very springtime you'll enjoy it night and day.

Paige Cameron (10)
New Elgin Primary School, New Elgin

Springtime

S pring is the best time of the year
P retty flowers come out from the grass
R abbits race from the woods to the fields
I n the garden is such a peaceful place to be in springtime
N ight is never ever seen
G reen grass growing out in the fields
T ime for mums and dads to do a tiny spring-clean
I t's just like springtime has never been seen
M arvellous time for the children to stay and play
E veryone's happy now that spring's sprung.

Jade Young (9)
New Elgin Primary School, New Elgin

Springtime

S pringtime is here. Get your feather dusters ready
   For your spring-cleaning.
P etals rising up - daffodils to lovely tulips sitting in the sun.
R acing rabbits at the speed of blazing lightning through the
   Tall grass.
I like to go out and play games in the brilliant days of spring.
G ardens bright with bluebells. Nice sunny time of spring.
T ime for spring again. Time for bluebells and daffodils to rise
   In the sun.
I n spring you can play games in the evening. Have a bike ride
   In the sun.
M ore sun each and every day. Some showers through for the
   Flowers to grow big and strong.
E very day flowers grow in the beautiful sunshine of great
   Springtime.

Greg Gallacher (10)
New Elgin Primary School, New Elgin

Springtime

S pringtime once again
P laying on long evenings
R acing bunnies in the fields
I n and out of their burrows
N ew animals being born;
G oslings, ducklings, chicks, fox cubs, foals, lambs,
   Calves, fledglings, owlets and piglets
T ime to spring-clean all over the house
I n and out of the cupboards and cobwebs everywhere
M any plants are growing in our garden
E njoy the beautiful colours on the plants.

Angela Adam (9)
New Elgin Primary School, New Elgin

Young Writers - Playground Poets - Inspirations From Scotland

Fear

Fear is a great white shark
It can snap you in two
Then swallow you whole
Don't get near or you're minced meat

Fear is a black widow spider
It can be small as well as big
It can eject poison into your skin
Squash it before it gets you!

Fear is all around you
Phobias of snakes, of darkness
Spiders, monsters, bugs and fish
Fear can scare you to *death!*

Drew Crawford (11)
Pennyland Primary School, Thurso

Sadness

Every Sunday night my uncle John
    Went down to the pub
        To get merry
            Just one Sunday night he got into a fight
He broke his arm and his leg.
    As soon as I heard, sadness fell to my heart
        I was holding onto my uncle John
            I wouldn't let him go
It's just one Friday, midnight - he died.
    Sadness fell to my heart one more time.
        Whenever a member of my family is in jeopardy
            I'll always be there for them.

Aaron Taylor (9)
Pennyland Primary School, Thurso

Darkness

Black darkness is a terrible thing,
It's not something smile can bring.
Deep darkness takes the road to pain,
It can drag you down like the rain.
Bad darkness is with you everywhere.
In your room and on the stair.
Evil darkness is a terrible thing,
There is no goodness it can bring.

Andrew McKay (10)
Pennyland Primary School, Thurso

Darkness

Darkness is black
It is like a dark cave
People on the streets at night
Usually mug you
Goblins in the mountains -
Ready to kill you
In the darkness.

Matthew Hardman (11)
Pennyland Primary School, Thurso

Hate

Hate is something you really don't like,
Such as baked beans, your brother or sister.
Sometimes hate happens when you're angry -
Or out of jealousy.
Sometimes hate causes war
All I know is that there is lots of hate in the world!

Cameron Laidlaw (10)
Pennyland Primary School, Thurso

Anger

Anger is evil and insane.
It makes you feel mad
It feels like lightning
Has come upon you
And makes you feel crazy,
Yet alone.
Colours come into your mind,
Like dark purple,
And dark blue.
It makes you feel
You need to fight.
When you are angry
You get really cross
And beside yourself
With rage!

Sarah Douglas (10)
Pennyland Primary School, Thurso

Anger

Anger is evil and the colour is dark purple.
When I get angry I feel like
I'm going to explode
With red-hot lava!
I could stamp my feet and make lightning.
I get mad and I'm angry,
Sometimes I break things,
And rip some things.
It's like getting the flu
When I've got anger in me
I have a really bad and big temper.

Hannah Smith (10)
Pennyland Primary School, Thurso

Anger

Anger is hot,
Hot as lava.
I don't know what to do,
I'm nearly at the top,
I'm boiling hot.

I'm going to turn violent,
I'm going to trash the place.
I'm just so angry!
It's just all too much for me
I can't handle it anymore.

My cheeks are steaming red,
There's lava coming out of my ears.
I need to cool down,
I need to go to the pool to chill.

But I'm too depressed
And I'm so angry,
I can't afford it,
So it looks like
I'll have to stay like this.

Gemma Mackay (10)
Pennyland Primary School, Thurso

Love

Love is happiness
Love makes my heart flutter
When I fancy a boy I dream I'm in Heaven
But then I wonder, *does he fancy me*
Or does he fancy someone else?
And then he comes up to me and says,
'Will you go out with me?'

Gemma Strange (10)
Pennyland Primary School, Thurso

Anger

Sometimes I feel happy,
Sometimes I feel sad;
But sometimes I feel anger
When things are bad.

Sometimes I feel worried,
Sometimes I feel surprise,
But sometimes I feel anger
When someone tells me lies.

Sometimes I feel lonely,
Sometimes I feel great,
But sometimes I feel anger
When the world is full of hate.

Fraser Baxter (9)
Pennyland Primary School, Thurso

Anger

Anger boiling up in me,
Burning, flaming and deadly,
Makes me feel like trashing stuff,
Sometimes I go in a huff,
I feel crazy, demented and insane,
I'm not able to stand the pain,
Now I must go and hide away,
And there forever I will stay,
Thinking about what I have done,
My anger still red-hot like the sun,
Waiting for my day to come,
When I will die my days are done!

Jack Dunnett (9)
Pennyland Primary School, Thurso

Happiness

Happiness, happiness
What will I do?
Everything is golden
Nothing is blue
Happiness, happiness
I'm over the moon
Higher than the sky
Hear the beautiful tune
Ecstatic I fly
Joyfully, cheerfully
Clouds moving by
Like a fluffy ice cream
In a happiness dream!

Amelia Mackay (9)
Pennyland Primary School, Thurso

Anger!

Anger is blood-red,
It makes me wish that I was dead.
It feels like flaming lava,
Bursting out of a volcano
I think I might turn violent.
Evil, I am furious,
I could turn mad
I feel dark
And deadly inside.

Stacey Fry (10)
Pennyland Primary School, Thurso

Hate

Hate, hate a nasty thing
It makes you miserable,
You don't want to sing.
It runs through your head,
It runs through your body,
It runs through your heart,
And through your tummy,
That hate.
To get rid of hate
Think of something good
One way is to think of -
Your favourite food.

Lewis Maclellan (9)
Pennyland Primary School, Thurso

Happiness Is . . .

Dancing
Cleaning my granny's house,
Annoying my brother,
Going on holiday,
Feeling the sun on my face,
Having barbecues,
And all the neighbours coming over.
Playing with my friends at home
Staying up late
Going down the town.

Leanne Maclean (9)
Pennyland Primary School, Thurso

Darkness

The black of midnight
Comes into my room,
Frightening shadows
Appear in the gloom.

The window bangs
The furniture creaks
My bed seems to move
And something squeaks.

Is something unpleasant
Hiding in my room?
Is my toy box turning
Into a tomb?

My room is scary
Dim and pitch-black
The door is open
The tiniest crack.

I lie trembling with terror
Unhappy and glum
I really *hate* darkness
I wish morning would come!

Ashley McPhee (11)
Pennyland Primary School, Thurso

Fear

Creeping and crawling,
Through the darkness.
Barbaric loud sounds up ahead
It sounds bloodthirsty
Roaring up ahead,
Will he kill me?
Am I going to die?

Jamie Lawrie (11)
Pennyland Primary School, Thurso

Fun

Fun, fun, amazing fun
What can we do without fun?
If there wasn't any fun in the world
We would just be sitting there being dumb
But who came up with the feeling? Not me,
But all I know is . . .
Fun is fun,
Fun is a feeling we can't hide
A feeling that shows outwards
But comes from deep inside.

Danielle Hawken (10)
Pennyland Primary School, Thurso

Happiness

H appiness
A lways happy
P ositive feelings
P ink is the colour of happiness
I n a happy mood
N ever sad
E lated and joyful
S oaring soul, skyward
S ometimes I just want to fly away.

Shannon Fulton (10)
Pennyland Primary School, Thurso

The Glass Tanka

Little liquids leap
Glistening gleaming glass glimmers
Broken brown bottles
Glass is as green as glitter
Bottles sparkle and shimmer.

Sam Berry (10)
Philiphaugh Community School, Selkirk

Glittering Glass

G littering glass glowing green
L iquids light as bubbles
A rrange your bottle collection
S mack, smash, shiny glass
S top, reduce and recycle at last.

Nicola Dehnolm (11)
Philiphaugh Community School, Selkirk

My Glass Poem!

G reen glass glistens fast
L ight gleaming, labels shiny
A round the world bottles smash
S hiny glass, coloured patterns
S mall, glistening, shiny glass.

Annabel Watson (10)
Philiphaugh Community School, Selkirk

Glass

G lass is green, clear and brown
L ids, labels and lights shine off the glass
A nd glass is sharp when they smash
S hattering glass can get in your eye
S mashing glass can be different shapes.

Danny Brown (11)
Philiphaugh Community School, Selkirk

Glistening Glass

Glistening glass gleams, glitters
Clear glass cracks smashes and bangs
Shiny glass sparkles and gleams
Re-use, recycle, reduce.

Stuart Hislop (10)
Philiphaugh Community School, Selkirk

Glass

G reen glass gleaming gently
L ots of liquids, labels, lids, light, sometimes heavy
A nd all the bottles smashed and cracked
S hatter, smash, crash, bang, in the bottle bank
S tart to recycle and save some glass.

Lee McCudden (10)
Philiphaugh Community School, Selkirk

Glass Tanka

Gleaming glass glistens
Smashed bottles shatter sadly
Clear bottles clatter
Bottles clatter, bang and break
Clear glasses clatter and crack.

Matthew Valentine (10)
Philiphaugh Community School, Selkirk

Sounds Of The Sea

The sea ripples like a river
And sounds like a sleeping cat.
It sways slowly side to side.

The sea roars like an angry lion,
It crashes like a blasting tiger,
It explodes through the sky like an eagle
It thrashes side to side
And moans like a baby.

Craig Wright (11)
Rockfield Primary School, Oban

Calm Sea

Softly swooping over and under, in and out
Softly and quietly going through the sand
Rippling and peacefully moving gently across with a soothing melody.
Cheerfully whistling a lullaby.

Thrashing and crashing into the walls.
Roughly smashing and splashing everyone
While it's screaming and shouting
Moaning and groaning and tearing everything apart
While raging and screeching and deafening everyone!

Lauren Smith (11)
Rockfield Primary School, Oban

Sounds Of The Sea

The calm sea moves gently along
Rippling over the smooth pebbles bubbling in the sand
So calm and peaceful, so silent and still
You can almost hear whispers in the wind
The swishing of the waves makes you relax
As if you are softly floating on top of the ocean.

Nicola Burgar (11)
Rockfield Primary School, Oban

Sounds Of The Sea

The whipping waves of the sea splash, roar and fizz.
An angry lion with a thundering roar!
As this thrashing beast explodes onto the shore.

A soothing calmness of the sea
Singing a gentle song.
No whips, no lashes, not even a squeak.
A peaceful motion that sounds so beautiful.

Aidan Harris (12)
Rockfield Primary School, Oban

Sound Of The Sea

The rough angry sea is like leaves in the wind
Splashing the rocks and thrashing the beach
Mashing the shells and ripping the seaweed
Like a hungry shark.

The calm gentle sea is like a tree in a light breeze swaying
From side to side
Relaxing on the seabed.
Bubbling softly and quietly
Rippling peacefully onto the sand.

Anna Smith (12)
Rockfield Primary School, Oban

Sounds Of The Sea

The quiet sea is singing a soft melody
So beautiful for our ears to hear
A peaceful song for it to sing
While it is softly swishing
It sits so still quietly rippling off the rocks.

The angry sea is exploding off the jagged rocks,
Fizzing up with unleashed temper.
Roaring ever so loudly it could make you scream!

Katy Melville (11)
Rockfield Primary School, Oban

Sounds Of The Sea

A calm rippling peaceful sea
Swishing quietly from side to side
As it soothes the shore
A still soft bubbling sea
Flows along the bay
As it whispers into the shore.

Pamela Macnab (11)
Rockfield Primary School, Oban

Calm Sea, Rough Sea

As tranquil as a sleeping baby quietly murmurs the gentle sea.
Swooping over the golden sand
Comforting as a friend when you need them most
Melodic as an orchestra
As sweet as a lullaby
A very calm sea!

Roaring like a wild animal
Whistling like the restless wind
Clashing like two cymbals coming together
Rummaging like a stray cat looking for a meal
The furious sea!

Marcus Ward (11)
Rockfield Primary School, Oban

Sounds Of The Sea

The sea silently heads towards the beach swooping in and out
Of the spaces.
It peacefully reaches the beach and crawls up the sand
And then slopes back down the rocks into the sea
And starts over again.

Moaning and bashing its way over the sea like a stampeding
Elephant tearing down anything in its path
Thundering towards the shore where it thrashes its heavy body
Against the rocks.

James Milligan (11)
Rockfield Primary School, Oban

Calm Sea, Rough Sea

Swooping and rippling onto the seashore
The sea whispers softly to you every day
Lying still most of the time and sleeping peacefully
Can you hear the silent flowing like a peaceful butterfly?
Can you hear the soothing sounds of its lovely song?

See and hear the sea crash, bash and thrash the rock
Ripping and moaning at everyone it sees
Exploding and splashing on the pebbles in the sea
How angry can it get?
It must be sad!

Chloe Brown (11)
Rockfield Primary School, Oban

The Calm Sea

The calm sea is a soothing sound with a tranquil echo.
It makes you feel peaceful with its relaxing lullaby sound.
You get a feeling you've been hypnotized
By the still comforting sound.
The sea has its own way of rippling through the sand.

Swooping through the sand as the sea passes
As the flowing silent wave curves softly and gently
Like the sunset rippling at the crack of dawn
Somehow the tranquil, gentle sea comes to an end.

Rebekah MacFarlane (11)
Rockfield Primary School, Oban

The Sea

A rough sea
An angry bashing against the rocks
Moans and screams, stirring the waves
A crash and a bash explode in the water
With the ripping and thundering sound
That they make.

A calm sea
A silent, still swish of a quietly mellow sea
Ripples and bubbles, *swoosh*
Towards the shore soothingly.

A mellow melody sings out loud
A beautiful song
Which makes a very soft and peaceful sound,
Like the sea coming over every single pebble
That is on the beach
And quietly making them rattle by themselves.

Rachel Broadfoot (11)
Rockfield Primary School, Oban

Sounds Of The Sea

Exploding into the deep sparkly sky above.
The waves go thrashing off the lonely rocks
Like a thundering, roaring, fizzing unleashed tiger
Whacking, cracking, bashing together, never resting
Till night like a pack of wild hunting wolves.

The sea is so gently comforting as it passes
Singing peacefully, whistling songs as it ripples and bubbles
Off the soft calming sand.
Swooping out and swishing over the glittery pebbles.

Rowen MacAskill (11)
Rockfield Primary School, Oban

Happiness

It sounds like angels singing hymns in Heaven.
It tastes like a holiday at a funfair.
It looks like a fluffy cloud in the sky.
It feels like a bar of chocolate touching my tongue.
It reminds me of my first holiday at Disneyland Paris.
It smells like a delicious sweety shop.
It is fluffy white like a small kitten.

Robbie Wood (8)
St Gabriel's RC School, Prestonpans

Happiness

It sounds like a superstar singing on a beach at night.
It tastes like an ice cream on a hot sunny afternoon
It looks like stars sparkling and shining with the moon at night
It feels like a lucky, magical Christmas Eve
It reminds me of my super-fun special birthday party
It smells like someone cooking an apple pie on a hot summer's day.
Its colours are pink, red, light blue, violet, yellow, orange, green,
Gold and silver.

Jade McAlpine (8)
St Gabriel's RC School, Prestonpans

Happiness

It sounds like a magic, fun holiday.
It tastes like a magic, fun birthday.
It feels like a jolly fun day.
It reminds me of the beautiful fun Easter Day.
It smells like super magic angels.
It is red, green and yellow.

Mikey Hamilton (9)
St Gabriel's RC School, Prestonpans

Happiness

It sounds like magic on Christmas Day
It tastes like eating Easter eggs at Easter
It looks like a lovely, wonderful shooting star at night
It feels like opening a super surprise birthday present
It reminds me of moons and stars sparkling in the night
It smells like all the different flowers like daisies and roses
It is red and yellow and pink and green,
Gold, silver and light blue.

Derryn Dryburgh
St Gabriel's RC School, Prestonpans

Happiness

It sounds like a bird chirping in the morning.
It tastes like something very sweet indeed.
It looks like a pretty group of butterflies flying.
It feels like nothing you can describe at all.
It reminds me of when I got my cat.
It smells like the nicest perfume in the world.
It is the most beautiful colours of the rainbow.

Paige Cummings (9)
St Gabriel's RC School, Prestonpans

Happiness

It sounds like a really magic super-duper Bonfire Night.
It tastes like a magic super-duper Easter egg with Smarties on the top.
It looks like a magic, lovely, beautiful birthday present.
It reminds me of a sparkling fairy.
It smells like a sparkling, enjoyable, fun holiday with lots of shows.
What colour is it?
It is black, gold, orange, blue, white, purple and shady green.

Liam Storrie (8)
St Gabriel's RC School, Prestonpans

Anger

It sounds like a stick of thunder and lightning
It tastes like a blazing volcano
It feels like a boiling hot star
It reminds me of a blazing lava rock
It looks like a boiling hot volcano
It smells like a shooting star
It is red, black, yellow and green.

Darren Halliday (8)
St Gabriel's RC School, Prestonpans

Sadness

It sounds like someone crying
It tastes like something rotten
It feels like something rough
It reminds me of when my little sister was crying
It looks like someone lonely and sad
It smells like fire
It is black, grey, dark blue, purple and green.

Nicollette Blair (9)
St Gabriel's RC School, Prestonpans

Happiness

It sounds like the beat of a violin on a spring morning
It tastes like a lovely banana split
It feels like you want to burst with laughter
It reminds me of a fantastic jolly birthday party!
It smells like someone cooking a gorgeous cake
It is pink, purple, yellow, orange, blue, red, violet and cream.

Erin Scott (9)
St Gabriel's RC School, Prestonpans

Anger

It sounds like sparks in the air.
It tastes like a very spicy curry.
It feels like burning hot lava.
It reminds me of a boiling shooting star.
It looks like a monster.
It smells like a sticky, rotten fish.
Its body is blue and black.

Chloe Fraser (8)
St Gabriel's RC School, Prestonpans

Happiness

It sounds like angels singing hymns.
It tastes like fruit in a bowl.
It looks like toys in my room.
It feels like my birthday when I was having fun.
It reminds me of the Tay River.
It smells like we are eating at a restaurant.
It is the colour of blue.

Declan Luby (8)
St Gabriel's RC School, Prestonpans

Happiness

It sounds like a bird singing
It tastes like a hot chocolate
It looks like a star
It feels like a flower
It reminds me of a baby
It smells like ice cream.

Tyler Byrne (9)
St Gabriel's RC School, Prestonpans

Anger

It sounds like boiling hot lava.
It tastes like thunder and lightning.
It feels like colourful, sparkling hot lava.
It reminds me of a fire storm.
It looks like a boiling hot star.
It smells like lava rocks.
It is pink, maroon, purple, yellow,
Red, black, blue, green, brown and orange.

Ryan Turner (8)
St Gabriel's RC School, Prestonpans

Anger

It sounds like a red-hot bursting volcano
It tastes like a hot spicy curry
It feels like a streak of lightning
It reminds me of tornadoes
It looks like a stormy tidal wave
It smells like steam coming out my ears
It is stripy red and black.

Stuart Tait (8)
St Gabriel's RC School, Prestonpans

Happiness

My happiness is the beat of music
It tastes like a jolly fun Easter
A beautiful sparkling sparkler
A jolly fun Christmas
A sunny fun day in Grand Canaria
Blue, yellow, gold, brown and black.

Joanne Clelland (8)
St Gabriel's RC School, Prestonpans

Happiness

It sounds like a quad revving
It tastes like a spicy chicken
It feels like a car with hydraulics
It reminds me of a clean sparkling Ferrari
It smells like a chicken curry
It is black, silver, gold, orange, red, green,
Yellow and black.

Kieran Cowan (9)
St Gabriel's RC School, Prestonpans

Anger

It sounds like red-hot blazing fire.
It tastes like steam coming out of my ears.
It feels like a hot burning cooker on fire.
It reminds me of a boiling, boiling shooting star.
It looks like an ugly old monster screaming.
It smells like a rotten carrot in the fridge.
It is baby light blue and a baby maroon.

Holly Bye (8)
St Gabriel's RC School, Prestonpans

Happiness

It sounds like me playing 'Amarilo' on my violin
It tastes like a chocolate bongo on a stick
It looks like a Christmas tree
It feels like a big bass drum
It reminds me of my birthday
It is red, yellow, green and pink.

Erin Connachan (9)
St Gabriel's RC School, Prestonpans

Happiness

It sounds like a pop star is singing,
It tastes like a strawberry cake
It looks like the moon is shining in the sky
It feels really hot in the kitchen
It reminds me of when I went on holiday with my mum
And dad and my little sister
It smells like some really beautiful roses
It is pink, orange, blue, purple, black, green and yellow.

Kayleigh Houston (8)
St Gabriel's RC School, Prestonpans

Anger

It sounds like a very hot meteor shower.
It tastes like spicy curry.
It feels like an earthquake.
It reminds me of when I was bad-tempered.
It smells like a very hot pie in a cooker.
It looks like thunder and lightning.
It is red, black, dark green, dark blue and purple.

Connor Horrocks (8)
St Gabriel's RC School, Prestonpans

Anger

It sounds like meteors hitting the ground
It tastes like a very spicy curry
It feels like a very stormy earthquake
It reminds me of an erupting volcano
It looks like boiling hot lava
It smells like ashes of fire
It is a hot blazing furnace in a volcano.

Adam Connolly (8)
St Gabriel's RC School, Prestonpans

Anger

It sounds like a spicy curry sizzling on a hot cooker.
It tastes like a red-hot chilli pepper in my mouth and a spicy curry
At the same time.
It feels like you have steam coming out of your ears in the middle
Of the war.
It reminds me of thunder and lightning and it was so bad it shook
The windows.
It looks like a blazing, burning hot sun.
It smells like lava rocks on top of a ginormous volcano.
It is red, a dark shade of orange, an even darker red and also

maroon.

Josie Adams (8)
St Gabriel's RC School, Prestonpans

Anger

It sounds like a really big hot volcano and a twister.
It tastes like a really spicy hot curry and a burning sun.
It feels like a really big stormy tidal wave and a hurricane.
It reminds me of a really big bursting volcano and lava rocks.
It looks like a big shooting star and a mud flow.
It smells like a big bonfire and shooting stars
It is pink, blue, yellow and purple.

Liam Tervet (8)
St Gabriel's RC School, Prestonpans

Anger

It sounds like a streak of lightning.
It tastes like a spicy, blazing hot curry.
It feels like a thunderstorm.
It looks like steam coming out of my ears.
It smells like a cheese and tomato pizza.
It is red, yellow and orange.

Patrick McLaren (8)
St Gabriel's RC School, Prestonpans

Happiness

It sounds like a magic sunny day.
It tastes like a magic, lovely Easter egg.
It looks like an angel on top of a lovely Christmas tree.
It feels like the magic stars and a lovely moon.
It reminds me of a wonderful, super holiday in the sun.
It smells like a lovely magic chocolate bar.
It is yellow, pink, violet and purple.

Louis McCabe (8)
St Gabriel's RC School, Prestonpans

Anger

It sounds like a dog barking
It tastes like a bar of chocolate
It feels like a rose
It remembers me as being good at school
It smells like mints and tatties
What colour is it?
Red and orange.

Samara Hunter (8)
St Gabriel's RC School, Prestonpans

Spring

I feel happy when spring is coming
The flowers are growing.
Some chicks are hatched from their eggs.
There are birds busy singing and building new nests.
Animals are coming out of hibernation.
I could even eat ice cream and chocolate.
The snow has gone and the sun is shining.
There is fresh air for me.
I feel a bit sad when spring is ending.

Josin Jose (8)
St John's Primary School, Blackwood

Spring

I feel happy when I know spring is coming
The birds are singing and building new nests
There are lots of flowers and lovely yellow daffodils
Newborn lambs stumbling in the fields
It's not too cold for ice cream
Chocolate eggs for us to eat
The snow has gone and the sun is shining
At last I can go out to play
Animals are out of hibernation
Easter is here just like spring
I don't feel any different from spring to summer
The schools have Easter holidays
I feel sad when I know spring is ending.

Sophia Glanville (8)
St John's Primary School, Blackwood

Spring

I feel happy when I know spring is coming.
At last I can go out to play.
The snow has gone and the sun is shining.
There are lots of flowers starting to grow.
There are more children playing and having lots of fun
Playing Easter egg hunts.
Birds are singing and chirping all day long.
Lambs are playing and jumping around the fields.
Rabbits are hopping everywhere you go.
And remember, spring is nearly over but summer is almost here!

Olivia Glanville (10)
St John's Primary School, Blackwood

Spring

I feel very happy when I know that spring is coming.
At last I can play football with my brother.
The snow is gone and the sun is coming.
There are lots of flowers and leaves are grown.
It's not too cold for ice cream, yummy!
Next Sunday I will get some eggs off of my family.
I will see rabbits hopping about, they look lovely.
Newborn chicks and lambs trying to walk, they are adorable.
Birds are singing.
Lots of chocolate eggs, I can't wait until Easter!
I can smell the chocolate.

Daniel Lafferty (8)
St John's Primary School, Blackwood

Spring

I feel safe when spring is coming, it is almost here.
So get here for spring.
All the flowers grow in the deep grass
All the good scents are go!
Most animals stop hibernating when spring gets all around.
It is not too hot, it's not too cold, the weather is just fine.
You can get something good like ice cream.
All the birds are tweeting, all the noise is good.
You can say, you can say, you can say so much about spring.
You can say, you can say, you can say so much about spring.

Sean Tierney (8)
St John's Primary School, Blackwood

Spring

I feel happy when I know spring is coming.
At last I can go out to play.
The snow has gone and the sun is shining,
I can eat eggs and ice lollies.
The flowers are growing.
The children are playing in the grass and they are
Playing in the trees
And the birds are making their nests.
I feel sad when spring is ending.
Summer is almost here.

Fraser Munro (9)
St John's Primary School, Blackwood

Spring

I feel happy when I know spring is coming.
At last I can get out to play.
The snow has gone and the rabbits are out hopping
About in the field.
The flowers are dancing to the beat of the sun.
All of the children are having fun.
There are lots of games to play when spring is near.
I feel sad when spring is ending.
But summer is almost here!

Michael Marra (9)
St John's Primary School, Blackwood

Spring

I feel happy when I know spring is coming
Birds sing as they are building new nests
You can smell freshly cut grass
Lots of flowers growing
You can taste hot cross buns
We get lots of Easter eggs.

Lee Hughes (8)
St John's Primary School, Blackwood

Spring

I feel alive when spring is coming.
At last I can go out to play.
Painting eggs pretty colours.
Foals, piglets, lambs and calves like playing about.
Lots of chocolate eggs for us and ice cream too.
Rabbits are hopping about in the fields.
The children like to jump for joy
When they hear that spring is ending
And summer is almost here.

Paula Lavery (8)
St John's Primary School, Blackwood

Spring

I feel happy when I know spring is coming.
Birds are singing while building their nests.
Children playing, laughing and dancing.
Flowers are forming nice and bright.
Not too cold for ice cream.
Buds on the trees.
Newborn lambs frisking in the fields.
I feel sad when spring is ending but
Summer is almost here.

Ben Gallacher (10)
St John's Primary School, Blackwood

Spring

I feel happy when I know spring is coming.
Spring is something when the flowers are coming and
The leaves are growing on the trees.
The animals are out of hibernation and the birds sing in spring.
It is not too cold and not too hot, the weather is just right.
The rabbits are out and I can go outside.
I like spring.

Saranne Hamilton (9)
St John's Primary School, Blackwood

Spring

I feel happy when I know spring is coming.
At last I can go out to play.
The snow is gone and the sun is shining.
There are lots of flowers starting to grow.
It's not too cold for ice cream.
Lots of chocolate eggs for us to eat.
Birds are singing, building new nests.
Newborn lambs stumbling in the fields.
I feel sad that spring is ending,
But summer is almost here.

Lee McInally (9)
St John's Primary School, Blackwood

Spring

I feel happy when spring is coming
Animals waking, dogs barking, birds singing,
Fresh air, green fields, blue skies.
Fresh fruit growing on the trees.
Grass growing, rabbits munching more and more.
Lambs hopping and jumping round the fields.
Birds making their nest.
Happy, cheerful spring is here.

Darren Dearie (9)
St John's Primary School, Blackwood

Spring

I feel happy when I know spring is coming
The snow is gone and the sun is shining
The birds are playing and singing
At last I can go out to play with birds and butterflies
Birds building new nests
It is not too cold for ice creams and ice lollies
Newborn lambs stumble around the fields.

Lisa Law (9)
St John's Primary School, Blackwood

In Your Shoes

If I were in somebody's shoes
I wonder who it'll be
If you were in somebody's shoes
It definitely wouldn't be me.

I could be in Humpty Dumpty's shoes
Falling off the wall
He was better off
Didn't have a life at all.

If I were in somebody's shoes
I wonder who it'll be
I would be in Baa Baa's shoes
Lazing in the grass on the other side of the gates
Playing with his mates.
Why would I want to be in someone else's shoes?
Because I'm not wearing any!

Kirsten MacDonald (9)
St Mary's RC Primary School, Bathgate

The Galaday

The Galaday is full of fun and excitement
There are some rides that you cannot go on
But I wish we could
I really like the food
At the Galaday there are flower girls
Keepers of the keys and lots more
Sometimes it has a floor
I also like the shows
But I have to change my clothes.

At the Galaday there are also bands
I have to wash my hands
In the Galaday there are things that I like
But I cannot hike
The Galaday, the Galaday, the Galaday.

Nicola Reynolds (8)
St Mary's RC Primary School, Bathgate

My Cat Socks

My cat Socks is very fast
My cat Socks is very fat
He is like a big fat dart
Going about the house.

My cat Socks is very cute
And he always goes out of the house
He is like a big fat dart
Going about the house.

My cat Socks always comes
When I call
He is really, really nice.
He is like a big fat dart.
Going about the house.

Andrew Shedden (8)
St Mary's RC Primary School, Bathgate

Plants

I can grow short
I can grow tall
I can even grow up the garden wall.

Growing here
Growing there
I can grow anywhere.

I can grow up
I can fall down
But always my roots stay in the ground.

What am I?
Plants.

Cormac Hughes (8)
St Mary's RC Primary School, Bathgate

My Dog Heidi

My dog Heidi is very cute
My dog Heidi is very fast
I love her, I love her
Heidi would never come last.

Heidi loves her frisbee
Heidi likes her ball
Heidi hates every other thing
And she comes when I call.

Heidi never runs away
Heidi always likes to play
I love Heidi in every way.

Louise Burns (8)
St Mary's RC Primary School, Bathgate

My Dog Mat

My dog Mat is funny and glad
To have an owner who laughs and laughs
My dog Mat runs and runs
To catch the ball for Mum
He sees the ball so he runs so fast
Before he blasts
He is fluffy, he is sweet,
He is cool, he is kind
He is friendly, and so cosy and warm
He is groovy and fun
But after all I'm sure he is trying to be first
Instead of last
I love my dog Mat so much.

Caitlin McKenna (8)
St Mary's RC Primary School, Bathgate

Whoosh, Bang, Sizzle

Whoosh goes a Catherine wheel
A colourful, sparkly wheel.

> *Whoosh, bang, sizzle*
> *Whoosh, bang, sizzle*

Bang goes the rocket, up it goes
Up and up and up then . . .
> *Bang!*
Lots and lots of colourful sparks
Falling from the sky.

> *Whoosh, bang, sizzle*
> *Whoosh, bang, sizzle*

Sizzle goes the Roman candle
Up into the sky, up go the sparks, green, red and blue
All around the park
Then falling as slow as petals from a tree onto the grass.

> *Whoosh, bang, sizzle*
> *Whoosh, bang, sizzle*

Lick, lick, I hear everyone all around
Licking toffee apples.

Eva Doolan (9)
St Mary's RC Primary School, Bathgate

My Bed

My bed's soft and cosy
How I would like to lie all day
My parents always say, 'You have school today.'
My bed's warm and snug
How I wish I could have five more minutes
My parents always say, 'You've football training today.'
How I want to stay in bed
I've got stupid school instead.
School is over, it's the weekend now
I can lie in bed all day now.

Kieran Boyle (8)
St Mary's RC Primary School, Bathgate

Friendly Friends

Friendly friends
My friend Sarah
Never seems to be bad
She's one of my friends
Always there when I'm sad
Friendly friends, friendship never ends.

Friendly friends
My friend Eva
Always in a cheer
She's one of my friends
Helps me with what I fear
Friendly friends, friendship never ends.

Friendly friends
My friend Marie
She's always in a laugh
She's one of my friends
She helps me with my maths
Friendly friends, friendship never ends.

Friendly friends
My friend Nicola
She's always there to help
She's one of my friends!
Even there when I yelp
Friendly friends, friendship never ends.

Lisa Manson (9)
St Mary's RC Primary School, Bathgate

The Joyful Teacher

My teacher loves to play
Even when the weather is wind and rain
But when she's sick and off
She seems to have a cough
But she still loves to play
In the wind and rain.

Daniel Copeman (8)
St Mary's RC Primary School, Bathgate

My Dog Rosie

My dog Rosie, she is my hero
She is gloomy
She is sweet
I love her
But she can be mean to me
Although she is still sweet
When I rest she is the best
When you come in
She is scared
You must be new.

Shanna Smith (8)
St Mary's RC Primary School, Bathgate

My Car

If I had a star I would wish for a car
It would be fast and very flash.
I would never crash for it would look like trash.

I would ride it every day
On my way I would say 'I love to speed!'

I will never crash my flash car.

Marie McLaughlin (8)
St Mary's RC Primary School, Bathgate

The Hungry Lion

Hungry lion, what shall you eat?
Perhaps a big piece of plump chicken meat?
No, no, no, I don't think so
Dog brain or hippo pie,
Or a piece of rat's eye?
Rhino legs or rabbit stew?
All I really want to eat is you.

Youssef Bel Abbes (8)
St Mary's RC Primary School, Bathgate

I Wish I Had An Elephant

I wish I had an elephant
I wish I had a dog
I wish I had a hog
I wish I had a frog

Which pet should I choose?
What about the frog?
No it's too slimy, it looks like the hog
What about the hog? No it looks like the dog
What about the elephant? Yes!

Robbie Copeman (8)
St Mary's RC Primary School, Bathgate

Autumn Leaves

On a cold autumn's day
I watch leaves sway
When I am playing with my ball
My brother kicks it in the hall
Autumn leaves, autumn leaves
The leaves fall off the trees
Some leaves are small
Some are tall.

Lee Thomson (8)
St Ninian's RC Primary School, Menzieshill

My Teddy Bear

My teddy bear is cuddly,
It always sits on the end of my bed,
It looks like a tiger,
It feels like fur,
It smells like powder,
But most of all it cuddles me.

Tori-Jade Hodgson (8)
St Ninian's RC Primary School, Menzieshill

My Home

Dundee is my home
It is a very nice place to live.
Some people call it 'Bonnie Dundee.'

Dundee has two wonderful bridges
Over the beautiful Silvery Tay.
There's also the famous ship The Discovery.

Scotland is my home country
It's a really gorgeous land
With its high rugged mountains
Its lowlands and sands.

I really love the place I live,
And everything that's in it.
I don't think I will ever leave
My home.

Stevyn Wilkinson (11)
St Ninian's RC Primary School, Menzieshill

My Home

My house has two beautiful gardens
My house is big, safe and warm
I'm glad that I live there.

Dundee is my hometown
It is very colourful, but
Covered with snow at the moment,
Dundee has lots of parks and things to do.

Scotland is my homeland,
With its mountains and glens
I never want to leave.

Kirstie McAulay (10)
St Ninian's RC Primary School, Menzieshill

When The Mini Beasts Went For Tea

The mini beasts went for tea,
To a restaurant called The Squashed Bee.
They had bats' wings,
And wasp stings.
Cats' tails and raw snails
They had cockroaches
(Which came with free brooches)
And they had giant slugs
Served in blue mugs.

They had mud pies,
In a sauce which smelt like pigsties.
Plus a witch's nose and frog toes
A ghost's ear,
Drenched in beer.
Also pumpkin tops,
Served with lollipops,
And a bag of jelly babies,
Followed by a big bill from a bat with rabies.

Olivia Marr (11)
St Ninian's RC Primary School, Menzieshill

My Horrible Meal

I went to the mini beast munch
To get something for my lunch
I had some toasted bees
They started to make me sneeze
After that I ate a bat that was all covered in cheese!

Followed by bat wings and terrible things
I ate a lot
A whole big pot
The waitress said '£12 pounds please.'
That's a deal!
And that's what I ate for my horrible meal.

Karli Webster (10)
St Ninian's RC Primary School, Menzieshill

My Home

Dundee is my home
It is a lovely place to be
It has such a lot of
Special places
For everyone to see.

From the top of the
Law Hill you can
See the lovely view
Of all the city of
Dundee.

Dundee on the River Tay
Is a lovely place to stay
Two bridges cross the
River Tay and that is
Busy every day.

Dundee has lots of things
To do leisure centres, parks,
Cinemas too.

Rachel Cameron (11)
St Ninian's RC Primary School, Menzieshill

My Home

My home is in Dundee,
My house is close to a big park
Where I go and play,
From my house I see The Law,
An extinct volcano that
Dundee is built around.

My home looks over the river,
There are two bridges crossing it,
The water is like a silver ribbon,
That's why it's called the 'Silvery Tay'
Dundee, city of discovery,
Is where I stay.

Cameron Conway (10)
St Ninian's RC Primary School, Menzieshill

My Home

Bonnie Scotland

Woolly sheep, cows
And all
Cockerels give us a
Morning call,
With rivers that are
Clear and blue
Highlands, lowlands,
Moorlands too.

Robert the Bruce,
Robert Burns
That shows how the
Clocks have turned
Bravery, poetry - we're
Famous for our
Victories.

The Discovery sailed
Far around
Nowhere else can it
Be found except
Dundee.

So this is my home
I don't stay here
Alone
But with my family,
Happily.

Elise Wilson (11)
St Ninian's RC Primary School, Menzieshill

My Home

Scotland in the United Kingdom
It's where I live,
It's my home,
It's where my friends and family are,
We live here happily.
William Wallace fought for our freedom.

Scotland doesn't have great weather,
But it is fun in the snow,
Throwing snowballs at my friends
And making lots of snowmen.

With its rocky mountains and heather covered glens
I love it here
Scotland - my home.

Josh Bray (10)
St Ninian's RC Primary School, Menzieshill

Autumn Leaves

When I am out to play,
I like watching the autumn leaves fall,
As they sway,
I hear the wind call.

As I see the leaves fading away
I like their colour, golden brown
I have seen lots today
As I see them falling down.

On an autumn's day
Some leaves are red
And some blow away
But some leaves are dead.

Kelsey Gowans (8)
St Ninian's RC Primary School, Menzieshill

The Fireworks Display

Looking into the sky
Blue rocket going zoom
Boom, bang, red, blue, yellow
Colours in the black sky.

Sparkler that sizzles
Blue, red, yellow
Red sparks falling
To the green grass.

The finale
Boom, bang, zoom
A big red love heart
In the sky.

Shaun Thain (11)
St Ninian's RC Primary School, Menzieshill

Autumn Leaves

Autumn leaves, why do you fall off the tree?
You spin around and fall on the ground on an autumn day
Why do you die?
Oh why? Oh why? Oh why?
Autumn leaves spin round and round
But why on the crumply ground?

Shaun Wilkinson (8)
St Ninian's RC Primary School, Menzieshill

My Teddy

My teddy bear is cuddly
It always stays with me
It feels like fur
It smells like perfume
But most of all it is mine.

Kayleigh Papendorf (9)
St Ninian's RC Primary School, Menzieshill

December

D ecember is a special month
E veryone enjoys Christmas
C hristmas carols sing
E verybody deserves presents
M ary is related to Christ
B e good at Christmas
E verybody needs a Christmas dinner
R eindeer pull Santa's sleigh.

Cameron McGregor (8)
St Ninian's RC Primary School, Menzieshill

February

F ebruary is a cold and rainy month
E ating pancakes is fun
B oring sitting in the house
R ainy days are not fun
U mbrellas you will need
A ll people wear coats so they don't catch a cold
R uby rings for Valentine's Day
Y oung children can't play.

Lucy Smith (8)
St Ninian's RC Primary School, Menzieshill

Anger

Anger sounds like a roaring fire,
Anger tastes like burnt charcoal,
Anger is black like a hole that never ends,
Anger reminds me of a red dragon from Hell,
Anger feels like smashing glass in my stomach,
Anger looks like a charging bull,
Anger smells like death in the middle of nowhere.

Mary Pearson (10)
Sciennes Primary School, Edinburgh

Fear

Fear reminds me of damp, dank dungeons,
People crying distant cries,
Whispering winds moaning in sorrow,
Creatures fearing what will happen tomorrow,
Rabbits bolting,
Stormy days,
Lightning cackling as he plays,
Witches brewing up their stew,
The sight of it would make you blue,
Wind billowing,
Trees thrashing,
Thunder and lightning together are crashing,
Haunted mansions,
Creaking doors,
Shrieking above the attic floor,
This is fear for evermore.

Amirah Ahmed (11) & Natalie Prosser (10)
Sciennes Primary School, Edinburgh

Sadness

Sadness sounds like nothing
Ringing in my ears,
Sadness tastes like sour sweet,
Lasting in my mouth,
Sadness is like snow
That bright white colour,
Sadness reminds me of pain,
When no one can help me,
Sadness feels like I'm empty inside,
Like no one truly loves me,
Sadness looks like a lion,
Stuck behind wrought iron bars,
Sadness smells like nothing
Nothing.

Kirstie-Ann McPherson (11)
Sciennes Primary School, Edinburgh

Laughter

Laughter sounds like family and friends
It tastes like joy and fun
Laughter is like a sunny blue sky
It reminds me of the sun
Laughter feels like love and peace
It looks like light and hope
Laughter smells like lavender plants
It feels like you can cope!

Mairi Cross (10)
Sciennes Primary School, Edinburgh

Sadness

Sadness sounds like a roaring lion,
Sadness tastes salty from the tears
Running down your face,
Sadness is the colour pale blue,
Sadness reminds me of loneliness and emptiness,
Sadness feels like you are lost and alone in the wilderness,
Sadness looks like you have no hope,
Sadness smells like a fresh painted room.

Sophie Devlin (10)
Sciennes Primary School, Edinburgh

Fun

Fun is when children laugh and play,
In the garden on a sunny day,
Fun is doing something you like
Listening to music or riding a bike.

Iain Brown (11)
Sciennes Primary School, Edinburgh

Happiness

Happiness sounds like a robin in the snow
Happiness tastes like a sweet polo
Happiness is the colour of pink clouds in the sky
Happiness reminds me of good steak pie
Happiness feels like buttercups and roses
Happiness is the colour of the rainbow
Happiness smells like a bright summer's day.

These are a few of our favourite things.

Richard Ellis, Toby McClorey (10) & Abdullah Muaqat (11)
Sciennes Primary School, Edinburgh

Darkness

Darkness sounds like rattling breath,
It tastes like rotting lemons,
Darkness is a sea of black
It reminds me of dark cold nights with werewolves
And witches creeping about.
Darkness feels like a wet, cold, foggy and damp night.
It looks like nothing,
Darkness smells like rotten milk.

Kirsten MacFarlane & Jonathan Robertson (10)
Sciennes Primary School, Edinburgh

Anger

Anger is dark red like pouring blood
It looks like a midnight storm
Anger smells like burning metal
It feels like an electric shock surging through your veins
Anger tastes like red-hot chillies burning your tongue
It sounds like drums beating in your ears
Anger reminds me of lava flowing from an erupting volcano.

Tom Walker, Oh-Heon Kwon (10) & Anna Purdom (11)
Sciennes Primary School, Edinburgh

The Scottish Mountain Climber

I can see the cliffs above my head
The snow on the mountains
The grey dim clouds

I can hear the rocks raining down the mountains
The soft raindrops hitting my head
The wind whistling
I can feel the freezing snow on my gloves.
The wind blowing my face and my woolly jumper.
I hope I reach the top.

Leon Miller (8)
Stobhill Primary School, Gorebridge

Vikings

I can see the curved dragon head and the calm sea
I can see the mountains that have snow on them
I can hear the swishing oars
I can hear people breathing so hard and us shouting,
'Hooray, hooray!'
Because we have just won a fierce battle.
I can feel my heart thumping -
I am scared that I might die
But I am brave and strong.

Samantha McColm (8)
Stobhill Primary School, Gorebridge

Love

Love is lavender like roses and violets
It sounds like the breeze in the air
It tastes like vanilla ice cream
It smells like my Labrador
It looks like my dad
It feels like ice cream
It reminds me of my nana.

Emma Cullen (8)
Stobhill Primary School, Gorebridge

Dancing

I can see other people dancing in front of me.
I can see my teacher talking.
I can see people looking in through the window.
I can hear music in my ears.
I can hear people talking.
I can hear people dropping mats.
I can feel my dress on me.
I can feel the mats on the floor
I am excited because it is nearly time for my show.

Paige Watson (8)
Stobhill Primary School, Gorebridge

Springtime

Bright spring leaves on the trees
Mums with their children going home
School bags on their backs

I can hear birds and closing doors
Eight children laughing

I can feel the heat on my face
And the wind too, pulling the grass
I am sitting on.

Dale Cummings (8)
Stobhill Primary School, Gorebridge

Happiness

Happiness is yellow like sunflowers in the garden
It sounds like blue tits tweeting outside
It tastes like melting ice cubes in your mouth
It smells like my Labrador's soft fur on his body
It looks like the golden sun in the blue air
It feels like the soft teddy my gran has
It reminds me of all the people in my family.

Abbey Rutherford (8)
Stobhill Primary School, Gorebridge

The Vikings

I can see mountains in the distance
And the curved dragon's head on the front
Of my long boat in the stormy, deep blue sea.

I can hear Vikings singing 'Hooray, hooray!
We have just won a fierce battle.'
There are seagulls screeching overhead.

I can feel my heart pumping.
I feel strong and powerful,
I'm glad that the battle is over,
I am going home now.

Chanel Drysdale (8)
Stobhill Primary School, Gorebridge

Love

Love is red like roses
It sounds like birds tweeting
It tastes like sweets and sugar
It smells like cola
It looks like two people kissing
It feels like summer
It reminds me of my papa.

Sam Fisher (8)
Stobhill Primary School, Gorebridge

Sadness

Sadness is grey in a rainstorm.
It sounds like misery.
It tastes like my mouth is burnt.
It smells like a house on fire.
It looks like disappointment.
It feels like glumness inside.
It reminds me of falling out with my friends.

Emma Wilson (8)
Stobhill Primary School, Gorebridge

Insect

I can see giants
I can see giant houses
I can see more insects
I can see long grass
I can hear cars
I can hear bees
I can hear the pond
I can hear people screaming
I can feel the leaves
I can feel my wings
I am a ladybird.

Chloe Hutchison (8)
Stobhill Primary School, Gorebridge

Anger

Anger is orange like steam
It sounds like a heavy rainfall
It tastes of hot fireballs on my tongue
It smells like an inferno and an explosion
It looks like red everywhere.
It feels like hot steam everywhere on me.
It reminds me of a house on fire.

Joel Urquhart (8)
Stobhill Primary School, Gorebridge

Love

Love is like the pinkness of the sky
It sounds like peaceful places
It tastes like raspberry ice cream
It smells like freshness in the air
It looks like red roses
It feels like the smoothness of a table
It reminds me of Valentine's Day.

Erin Flanagan (8)
Stobhill Primary School, Gorebridge

The Vikings

I can see the stormy deep blue sea and
A mountain in the distance.

My map is in front of me
Showing me the way to go.

I can hear the wind and the water smashing
Off the rocks and the splashing of the oars.

I can feel my heart thumping,
I'm very scared because we are getting closer to the land.
I might die, but I'm brave and strong.
I can feel my silver brooch and my furry cloak keeping me warm.

Rachel Robertson (8)
Stobhill Primary School, Gorebridge

Viking Warriors

I can see the deep blue sea
I can see other people on the boat.
I can see my sword at the side of me.
I can see the mountains in the distance.
I can hear the waves swishing all around me.
I can hear Vikings singing 'Har har
We've just won a battle.'

I feel very brave.
The wind is blowing against my face
I feel very strong
I can feel my furry cloak wrapped around me.

Lori McVittie (8)
Stobhill Primary School, Gorebridge

An Aeroplane In The Sky

I am sailing in the sky
I can see everybody below me
It is such fun
I hope they can see me.
I can hear the cars and the long trains
Oh! There's one!
This is such fun with all these passengers on me.
Oh! That tickles!
I can do anything!
I can turn around like this.
It is so much fun.
I wish you could do it!
Even though I have toys which are my window wipers,
I wanted them to be on human eyeballs because then
They will be able to clean them.
And I love feeling the air in my eyes.
I can feel clouds, smoke,
And space up above me.
I can feel my engines running
I can feel that I am slowing down
I just hope the pilots put my wheels out,
Because I don't want to die and kill all these people
And fail my mission.
Ha, ha, I feel seat belts tickling me,
Footsteps walk away from me.

Cole McCulloch (8)
Strone Of Cally Primary School, Bridge of Cally

The View Of A Pine

I can see hundreds and thousands of trees
I can see a bear walking below me.
There is an eagle making a nest in my tree.
A squirrel has been putting cones in my trunk.
The nest now has a few eggs in it.
I can see a little boy picking up cones.
I can also see families having picnics.
At the top of my tree there is a hive of bees.
I can feel a lynx scratching at my trunk.
A bear is hanging off my favourite branch.
Snap the bear falls to the ground with a thump.
Something is missing, I look down and my branch is gone.
It is laying on the ground with the beehive.
I can see my friends being chopped down on the horizon.
I can feel something that I don't want to feel.
I feel that I am going to die.
I feel the wind rubbing my branches together.
I can see and hear a chainsaw.
My friends are gone, quick, wow!
One more tree till I'm going down.
I can feel an axe hacking at my trunk.
We are all gone but our spirit lives on.
The salmon will still leap.
The birds will still cheep,
We will make way for a new generation.
There was a Norway made in this forest.
It was the last in Scotland, it is now gone.
This place will become marshland.
Chop! I am gone.

Connor Blanche (11)
Strone Of Cally Primary School, Bridge of Cally

The Environment

What can you see?
What can you feel?
What can you hear?

Bear.
I can see a bear in the river catching salmon with her cub.
I can hear other cubs lying down in the tall, tall grass.
I can see an adult male in a tree licking honey.
The adult bear comes down and emerges from the trees.
The male bear runs after the cubs and chases them into the forest
growth.

The mother bear called Sarah calls for her cubs.
No answer.
She tries again as her cubs cry.
I can feel that I am lucky to have my cubs.
I can feel that I am going to shed tears.
I can feel that my cubs have a chance of surviving in the wild.
I can feel something rushing towards me.
It gets closer every step.
I can hear the rustle where it steps.
It gets closer and closer.
I can hear it run straight at me.
I run and run as fast as I can.
I stop and look back to see if it is gone.
It isn't, so I run with my cubs.
I try and hide with them.
It is a man. He gets his gun out,
Bang, bang, bang,
We're extinct.

William Blanche (9)
Strone Of Cally Primary School, Bridge of Cally

Ancient Egypt

I can see the prisoner in the middle of the chasm.
I hear him whimpering and pulling at his chains
I can feel his fear that makes my blood run cold,
I can see the hand axe in my hand,
I can hear the whispering of the crowd,
I can feel my breath vibrating around the room,
I hear the priest saying that if I do this I will become a pharaoh.
I can see the bloody panic-stricken face.
I see myself raise the axe and bring it down on his neck.
I hear the chop and the head and blood splatter to the ground.
I feel the vibration of the head and body thumping to the ground.
I hear the roar of the crowd and the priest saying 'Well done.'
I see everyone stand up and leave the chasm.
I can feel myself quake and quiver,
I can see the light dim.

Harris McCulloch (9)
Strone Of Cally Primary School, Bridge of Cally

War Poem

As I see the German tanks approaching me
I am quaking in my boots in fear
That I might get shot.
I can see the German planes soaring overhead
And can see the German flag.
I can also see the raging soldiers charging towards me.
I can hear the rapid gunfire as bullets whizz across my nose.
I can hear tanks and explosions as I seek cover in the trenches.
I can hear the cries of yelling men as they are brought down
One by one.
I can feel sand hitting my face
I can feel wind blowing against my face.
I can feel bullets skimming my body.
I can feel a pain in my head.

Callum Rimmer (9)
Strone Of Cally Primary School, Bridge of Cally

Mr Wolf

When I, a cub, get brought into this cold, snowy world
In a warm, earthy den, I see fellow cubs scrambling,
Trying to get milk.
When the youngest, that's me, gets pushed to the bottom
In the surge to get milk
I don't get much, but this does not dishearten me.
For I can still live on a small amount of food.
As years go by I play with my brothers and sisters.
The love of my mother gives me food.
I'm nearly old enough to leave but not quite!
So this is anger and bitter sadness!
This spiteful bear shall feel my wrath.
Dark thoughts shatter my mind to leap through the forest.
To face the killer of my mate, my mother, my brothers and sisters,
And my cubs!
Bear fight with me. The glinting yellow eyes stare at me
With a roar and a snarl we launch towards each other.
With a whirl of fur I fall wounded, the bear trips over a root.
I hear the sound reverberate.
Is this death? Farewell
You'll find me in the Arctic now, bye!

Lewis Crichton (9)
Strone Of Cally Primary School, Bridge of Cally

Who Loves Me?

Who reads me a story when I'm snuggled in my bed?
Who takes my covers off?
Who puts Bugs Bunny up my nightie?
Who brushes my hair?
Who loves me?
My mum!

Kiera McKimm (6)
Whitecross Primary School, Whitecross

Children In The Playground

Children in the playground,
Children in the playground
Jumping up and down
And falling to the ground,
Children small and running fast,
Children laughing all the time,
It's fun to play in the playground.

Craig Lang (7)
Whitecross Primary School, Whitecross

The Worst Thing To Do In The Playground

The worst thing to do in the playground
Is to ask to play and they say no.
I am all alone.
There is one more person left to ask
And they say yes!

Cameron Marshall (7)
Whitecross Primary School, Whitecross

The Worst Thing To Do In The Playground

The worst thing to do in the playground
Is to be last in the line
When it is snowing.

Iain Parkinson (7)
Whitecross Primary School, Whitecross

Who Loves Me?

Who buys me toys?
Who gets me DVDs for Christmas?
Who tucks me into my bed?
Who kisses me on my cheeks?
Who loves me?
My mum!

Steven Ramage (7)
Whitecross Primary School, Whitecross

Children In The Playground

Children in the playground,
Children in the playground,
Merry, happy, noisy children,
Friendly, fast, funny children,
Laughing until your cheeks go red,
Running when the bell goes.

Kevin Struthers (7)
Whitecross Primary School, Whitecross

The Worst Thing To Do In The Playground

The worst thing to do in the playground -
Is to be playing a special game
When the bell goes!

Chelsea Forbes (6)
Whitecross Primary School, Whitecross

Children In The Playground

Children in the playground
Children in the playground
Hoppy, skippy, jumpy children
Happy, tired, small children
Giggling and laughing, filling the playground
With echoes - it's so good to have a friend.

Fiona Parkinson (7)
Whitecross Primary School, Whitecross

Children In The Playground

Children in the playground
Children in the playground
Jumping, running, skipping children
Noisy, loud, sniffy children
Singing and dancing children
I like it in the playground.

Georgia Brodie (6)
Whitecross Primary School, Whitecross